Lincoln In Louisville

A Play in Two Acts

By
David S. Traub, Jr.

Cover Design by Joey Arena

ISBN 978-1-7347313-8-5

academyartspress.com

All Rights Reserved.
Copyright © 2020 by David S. Traub, Jr.

DAVID S. TRAUB, JR.

Lincoln In Louisville

CAST

Joshua Speed	27, plantation owner & friend of Lincoln
Abraham Lincoln	32, lawyer and legislator
Mary Speed	39, Joshua's half-sister
Lucy Speed	53, matriarch of the Speed family
Morocco	26, a field slave at Farmington
Rose	36, the Speed family's house slave
Hiram Bracker	48, overseer at Farmington
James Speed	29, Joshua's older brother
Anton Heinrich	63, a traveling composer

For royalty information and permission to use this play in a performance, please email vin@academyarts.com with the following information:

Theater Name, City & State
Production Dates & Number of Performances
Ticket Prices & Number of Seats
School, Community Theater or Professional Company
Artistic Director and Contact Information
We will contact you promptly by email with Author's Permission & Royalty Information

Suggested music for the play will be provided by the playwright upon request

Lincoln In Louisville

Prologue

Act One

Scene One	In front of Farmington Manor
Scene Two	At the Dinner Table
Scene Three	In front of Lincoln's Bedroom
Scene Four	In the Basement Kitchen
Scene Five	On the Front Porch
Scene Six	Downtown Louisville
Scene Seven	In front of Farmington Manor

Act Two

Scene One	In front of Farmington Manor
Scene Two	Rose's Cabin
Scene Three	In the Speed parlor

Epilogue   The White House

Prologue

AT RISE. Lights slowly rise on a closed curtain, as JOSHUA SPEED *steps into the spotlight. He is a stocky man of 67, with the weight of the world creasing his face. His period clothing indicates he is a comfortably wealthy man in the late 19th Century, but not one given to finery or excess in his clothing. He stands before the closed curtain and addresses the audience.*

JOSHUA SPEED. It's hard to imagine how many years have passed since I was a young man eager to make my way in the business world. My friends, you know I no longer live at Farmington. Even my departure from that beautiful mansion off the Bardstown Pike seems long ago. That once I was a plantation owner, is inconceivable. Ahh. I can't forget that there were those fifty slaves working at Farmington. I never thought I could do without them. God knows how I've been able to adjust? Now I have this fine house in the city. Look around this room with its finery and gilt framed family portraits. You are sure to notice that I have prospered. That was because I shifted my sights to investments in real estate, in the railroads and, yes, I served on the boards of some big corporations. Listen…I can tell you I am proud of my contributions to civic life in Louisville. In this year of 1881, I am amazed how our United States has become such a different place from the one I once knew. Down here on the edge of the South, we've turned our attentions to a wider world. Yet, looking back on my life, nothing seems more memorable than a happening of forty years ago. In August of 1841, unforgettably, someone visited my home, a friend who had already made an impression. What I couldn't have imagined was what unusual events were to unfold…

LIGHTS FADE

ACT ONE, Scene 1

AT RISE. Lights come up before a small wooden gate with the stately Farmington Manor rising in the background. It is a warm Kentucky day in the summer of 1841. Joshua Speed stands with his gruff and plainly dressed overseer, HIRAM BRACKER.)

HIRAM BRACKER.   You might have been mistaken sending him to fetch Mr. Lincoln at the docks.

JOSHUA SPEED.   MOROCCO.   has served me well.

HIRAM BRACKER.   He's three hours late.

JOSHUA SPEED.   That's unlike Morocco.

HIRAM BRACKER.   He's a lazy one.

JOSHUA SPEED.   Maybe if you treated Morocco better.

HIRAM BRACKER.   Treat him better? I mean no offense, but you have some things to learn.

JOSHUA SPEED.   That may be.

HIRAM BRACKER.   Comes with time.

JOSHUA SPEED.   You've been here a long time, but...

HIRAM BRACKER.   I do my job.

JOSHUA SPEED.   I'm not so sure.

HIRAM BRACKER.   Your father was pleased with me.

JOSHUA SPEED.   That's something I can't know.

HIRAM BRACKER.   Times are different.

JOSHUA SPEED.   What do you mean?

HIRAM BRACKER.   The new plantations springing up round here...competition.

JOSHUA SPEED. You can deal with it.

HIRAM BRACKER. Only by being tough. If I'm not, the slaves will...well, just last week they broke a plow.

JOSHUA SPEED. Were you keeping an eye on them?

HIRAM BRACKER. Of course, I was.

JOSHUA SPEED. So there's another expense. One more thing to worry about. Mother wanted me to come back after father died. Now I understand why. I was having business troubles in Illinois. Oh, gosh were there aggravations, but there are even more down here.

HIRAM BRACKER. I can handle it, Mr. Speed.

JOSHUA SPEED. You say that. But can you handle my mother?

HIRAM BRACKER. I have great respect for Mrs. Speed. I surely do.

JOSHUA SPEED. As do I, Bracker, but she's used to a certain way of life.

HIRAM BRACKER. She's is a lady who deserves it.

JOSHUA SPEED. She's never known anything else.

HIRAM BRACKER. Then there's Miss Mary...

(A pause. Joshua turns to Bracker with suspicion.)

JOSHUA SPEED. What are you trying to say?

HIRAM BRACKER. Oh, nothing, Mr. Speed, I am sorry. Really it's none of my business.

JOSHUA SPEED. I'm just concerned Mary will never find a husband.

HIRAM BRACKER. She is a comely one.

JOSHUA SPEED. But getting older.

HIRAM BRACKER. Come to think of it she might be with us on the plantation for a while.

JOSHUA SPEED. Don't need your opinions.

HIRAM BRACKER. You've got to face facts.

JOSHUA SPEED. Bracker!

HIRAM BRACKER. Women want to get married. That's the way of things. Speaking of the women, I do confess I have a soft spot for them. You know that slave, Rose, is a good looker, I guess that's why I try to be nice to her.

JOSHUA SPEED. Damn it, Bracker. Don't let me ever hear that kind of talk. You keep your eyes…and your hands…off of her.

HIRAM BRACKER. Yes sir.

JOSHUA SPEED. I see Rose works her fingers to the bone. But my mother seldom appreciates her efforts.

HIRAM BRACKER. That's true, Mrs. Speed don't often have a kind word for Rose.

JOSHUA SPEED. Forget Rose. Your one concern is keeping your mind on the crops, remember harvest time is coming in a few weeks.

HIRAM BRACKER. And you want bails of hemp sent to those markets downtown.

JOSHUA SPEED. That's exactly what I want.

HIRAM BRACKER. I know sir. But being nice to a rotten slave like Morocco is not the way.

(Pause.)

JOSHUA SPEED. You have made that abundantly clear, Bracker. You deal with him as you see fit. But my rule still stands. There shall be no whippings at Farmington.

HIRAM BRACKER. Yes, sir.

JOSHUA SPEED. I mean what I say.

HIRAM BRACKER. As you wish, Mr. Speed.

(Bracker starts off, then stops at the gate)

HIRAM BRACKER. *(CONT'D.)* I think I hear the carriage.

JOSHUA SPEED. At last.

HIRAM BRACKER. So you'll be seeing Mr. Lincoln soon.

JOSHUA SPEED. I should have just gone to meet Abraham myself.

(MOROCCO enters, carrying luggage with a downcast Lincoln following. He is a solidly build African-American in clean but frayed slave clothing.)

ABRAHAM LINCOLN. Speed.

JOSHUA SPEED. You're here!

(They embrace.)

ABRAHAM LINCOLN. There were moments I felt I couldn't make the trip. It was such a struggle to just pack my bags.

JOSHUA SPEED. I know you have been down. Lord knows, I saw it for myself. But with a few weeks here, you'll get all of those ill thoughts out of your mind. I am certain of it.

ABRAHAM LINCOLN. Just sharing our friendship again will lift my spirits.

JOSHUA SPEED. Oh, that's good to hear.

HIRAM BRACKER. Morocco, what took you so long fetching Mr. Lincoln?

MOROCCO. Sorry, Mr. Bracker. I drove Mr. Lincoln back as soon as he came down the plank.

JOSHUA SPEED. We were waiting for three hours, Morocco.

MOROCCO. Master Speed, the steamboat was late.

HIRAM BRACKER. *(to Morocco)* I don't believe it. I'll bet you were dawdling on your way downtown, like you always do.

MOROCCO. The steamboat was late. It's the God's honest truth, Mister Bracker. I swear it was.

HIRAM BRACKER. Don't you lie to me, boy!

JOSHUA SPEED. Bracker, There was that storm last night, maybe there was trouble down on the river.

ABRAHAM LINCOLN. Yes, that storm. Indeed the boat was late.

HIRAM BRACKER. This ain't none of your concern.

JOSHUA SPEED. Bracker!

HIRAM BRACKER. Well, maybe the boat was a bit late, but not that late. *(Pause.)* As I say, let me do my job, Mr. Speed

(Speed waves him off. Bracker pushes Morocco offstage.)

HIRAM BRACKER. Boy, don't think you're not going to be punished for this.

ABRAHAM LINCOLN. Was that necessary, Joshua?

JOSHUA SPEED. Bracker troubles me. but Abraham, try to understand, I am the new one here. So far, I've tried not to interfere too much.

ABRAHAM LINCOLN. I suppose that makes sense.

JOSHUA SPEED. Living in Illinois for so long, I pretty much forgot about what goes on at a plantation. But as far as I know things like this don't happen often.

ABRAHAM LINCOLN. I am relieved to hear that.

JOSHUA SPEED. We do try to be as kind as we can be with the slaves and make sure that the overseer is as well. I don't know that I always succeed, but certainly we never whip them.

ABRAHAM LINCOLN. I have to admit, I know little of slavery. Ten years ago, I saw the slave markets down in New Orleans. Didn't like what I saw, but I've given the matter little thought since.

JOSHUA SPEED. And so you shouldn't. Don't concern yourself with my troubles. This is your time to rest.

ABRAHAM LINCOLN. Agreed. Let's forget all of this, and enjoy the few weeks we have together.

JOSHUA SPEED. That's the spirit! *(Throws his arm over Lincoln's shoulder.)* I was worried after your illness this past January.

ABRAHAM LINCOLN. You have to know it was a challenge getting back to my seat in the legislature. But when you left Springfield, in March I started getting depressed all over again.

JOSHUA SPEED. Maybe I shouldn't have left, but as you see, I came back here to challenges of my own. *(Places his hand on Lincoln's shoulder.)* Lincoln, you do look tired.

ABRAHAM LINCOLN. I must. I slept fitfully last night...one dream after another. The last one was so frightful. I dreamt we would never meet again. In a cold sweat, I awoke to thoughts that rushed through my mind like a tempest. *(Pause.)* Then there was a storm out on the river. Rolling waves tossed the boat back and forth... As we approached the canal at daybreak, the waters calmed. Before I knew it, we were at the levee, and yes, Morocco was there waiting.

(Pauses as if reflecting on the dream)

JOSHUA SPEED. Oh forget that silly dream.

ABRAHAM LINCOLN. A silly dream, perhaps. You know, I have learned to take note of them.

JOSHUA SPEED. You have always been a bit superstitious.

ABRAHAM LINCOLN. So many sad things have happened. I fear it was all intended.

JOSHUA SPEED. Life can switch around on you in an instant. Look, a year ago I didn't think I would be a slave master. *(Sadly.)* Then father died.

ABRAHAM LINCOLN. A far cry from running a general store.

JOSHUA SPEED. That's what I mean.

ABRAHAM LINCOLN. And for me, seeing a beautiful house like yours is something I wouldn't have imagined.

(Lincoln and Speed look toward the house.)

JOSHUA SPEED. Oh, look here comes, mother...and sister, Mary.

(LUCY SPEED walks briskly toward the gathering, with her daughter MARY in her wake. Lucy is the matriarch of the family and carries that proud responsibility in her walk and dress. Mary, by contrast, wears a less ornate white dress and reveals a slight hesitancy in her step. She looks up shyly at Lincoln, enamored of the stories she has heard about the tall stranger.)

JOSHUA SPEED. *(CONT'D.)* Mother, Mary, here is my friend Abraham Lincoln.

LUCY SPEED. Welcome to Kentucky and to our Farmington.

MARY SPEED. Yes, Mr. Lincoln, we are so glad you have come.

ABRAHAM LINCOLN. Well, thank you both for your welcome. And Mrs. Speed, before we go on, let me extend my condolences upon your loss.

LUCY SPEED. I am grateful for your saying that. I do really miss my dear departed husband John.

ABRAHAM LINCOLN. I am sure he was quite the gentleman. *(Turns to Mary.)* Miss Mary, I see you have Joshua's gracious smile and keen eyes.

MARY SPEED. How kind of you to say, Mr. Lincoln.

LUCY SPEED. Anyway, I know it was a long journey.

ABRAHAM LINCOLN. Yes and I do feel worn by it. I hope it doesn't show.

LUCY SPEED. Well it does a bit.

MARY SPEED. Mother!

ABRAHAM LINCOLN. I wanted to look my best.

LUCY SPEED. I don't mean to be discourteous, Mr. Lincoln, but I'll have Rose iron your suit. It is awfully rumpled.

MARY SPEED. Oh, mother.

ABRAHAM LINCOLN. No, Mrs. Speed, I appreciate that. It's the only one I have.

JOSHUA SPEED. You know, I've told you a bit about Abraham, but you've got to meet him in person. Yes, he is from Kentucky, still he's not quite like us at Farmington.

LUCY SPEED. I don't know what you mean.

MARY SPEED. Please, let Joshua explain.

JOSHUA SPEED. You've heard the story about Lincoln walking into my store with nothing but a saddle bag.

ABRAHAM LINCOLN. I guess I was quite a sight.

JOSHUA SPEED. 'Forlorn' would be the word I would use.

ABRAHAM LINCOLN. I was starting a new venture in the law. I was far from certain it would succeed.

MARY SPEED. You were stepping into the unknown.

JOSHUA SPEED. But you know, I saw something in Lincoln that I could relate to.

LUCY SPEED. Just what might that have been?

MARY SPEED. Mother, Joshua has always had good instincts about people.

JOSHUA SPEED. Well maybe, but I saw something unusual in Abraham. He was like the common folk, but then... that mind of his!

MARY SPEED. We look forward to seeing that mind come to life.

LUCY SPEED. Oh come, come. Let's show Mr. Lincoln the house.

JOSHUA SPEED. Back in Springfield I tried my best to describe the house to Abraham. I am not sure I did it justice.

(The group starts to walk toward the porch. Lincoln stares up at the house and looks to the ground in a down-cast way.)

MARY SPEED. What's the matter Mr. Lincoln? You seem preoccupied.

ABRAHAM LINCOLN. A thought came to mind...

JOSHUA SPEED. Always the troubled thoughts...

MARY SPEED.   What were you thinking, Mr. Lincoln?

ABRAHAM LINCOLN.   Oh. I was reminded of some matters left unfinished back home.

JOSHUA SPEED.   Abraham worries about things that don't trouble others.

MARY SPEED.   Well, he is sensitive, and that's a good trait.

ABRAHAM LINCOLN.   I tell myself, in a beautiful place like this, not to be burdened by the past.

JOSHUA SPEED.   Lincoln, enjoy it while you can. Soon enough, I'll be expecting to join you when you return to Springfield in September. I need to collect the money owed me from the sale of the store.

ABRAHAM LINCOLN.   I would be delighted if you joined me on my trip back.

JOSHUA SPEED.   Keep in mind I can't stay long in Springfield. Mother wants me back in time for the harvest.

LUCY SPEED.   That's right. Farmington cannot run itself. But enough for now, it's time to let Rose show Mr. Lincoln the room we've set aside for him. That one on the corner of the house.

ABRAHAM LINCOLN.   *(Wryly.)* You mean to say I get a room of my own?

LUCY SPEED.   You surely do.

ABRAHAM LINCOLN.   That will be the first time in my life.

MARY SPEED.   I can understand your pleasure in that. Joshua did tell me that you shared a room back in Illinois.

ABRAHAM LINCOLN.   True enough.

MARY SPEED.   That was smart, Mr. Lincoln. You didn't have to rent a place for yourself.

ABRAHAM LINCOLN.   And sharing that room did give us a chance to do a lot of talking.

LUCY SPEED.   Even as a child, Joshua loved to talk.

MARY SPEED.   I'll bet you two shared some confidences.

JOSHUA SPEED. So we did.

ABRAHAM LINCOLN. Speed, remember those winter nights sitting with our friends around the stove in your store. We sure stirred up a kettle of mirth.

JOSHUA SPEED. Lincoln, don't be modest; you were the center of attention with your yarns.

ABRAHAM LINCOLN. Well, maybe I was. Telling a funny story always gives me lift.

MARY SPEED. Why, tell us one.

ABRAHAM LINCOLN. All right. I have been feeling lately like I once did after I met a woman riding horseback in the woods. As I stopped to let her pass, she also stopped, and stared at me intently, said: "I do believe you are the ugliest man I ever saw." Said I, "Madam, you are probably right, but I can't help it!" "No," she said, "you can't help it, but you might stay at home."

(Everyone but Mary breaks into laughter.)

MARY SPEED. Oh, Mr. Lincoln, that's not funny. I think you are a nice looking man.

ABRAHAM LINCOLN. I appreciate the compliment Miss Mary. But I see no harm in poking a little fun at oneself now and then.

LUCY SPEED. No, you should have a more positive view of yourself.

ABRAHAM LINCOLN. That's what my physician, Doc Henry tells me.

MARY SPEED. Please, please, let Mr. Lincoln have some rest.

ABRAHAM LINCOLN. I am ready for that.

LUCY SPEED. Rose, come out here!
   (Rose enters from the house.)

LUCY SPEED. (CONT'D) Rose, this is our house guest, Mr. Lincoln.

ABRAHAM LINCOLN. So this is the Rose I have heard about.

ROSE. I am, sir.

LUCY SPEED.   Rose, take Mr. Lincoln to his room.
    (She points again to the room on the left side of the house again)
ROSE.   Yes ma'am. Mr. Lincoln, come with me, please.
    (Lincoln follows Rose into the house. The stage darkens.)

LIGHTS FADE

ACT ONE, Scene 2

AT RISE. Inside the well-appointed Farmington House. A corner of the stage is lit. Stage lights catch Lincoln and Rose Stage Right, standing before the guest room door.)

ROSE. You like your room Mr. Lincoln?

ABRAHAM LINCOLN. More than you can imagine.

ROSE: I'm mighty pleased.

ABRAHAM LINCOLN: Rose, tell me, have you been here long?

ROSE. Why do you want to know?

ABRAHAM LINCOLN. Curious.

ROSE. I don't like to talk about it.

ABRAHAM LINCOLN. Really, I would be interested to know.

ROSE. I never talk about such things with white folks.

ABRAHAM LINCOLN. I would like to think I'm a little different than most.

ROSE. Uh... Mr. Lincoln, I was born here.

ABRAHAM LINCOLN. Oh, I see.

ROSE. I was brought up with Master Speed. 'Course, he's been away for a while.

ABRAHAM LINCOLN. Might you be happy he's back?

ROSE. Doesn't change things for me.

ABRAHAM LINCOLN. Why do you say that?

ROSE. My two children were sold over at Cheapside Market in Lexington to a master from Mississippi.

ABRAHAM LINCOLN. Sad to hear that.

ROSE.   Oh I miss them so bad.

ABRAHAM LINCOLN.   You know I have a lady friend back home, Miss Todd from Lexington. She never mentioned the slave market.

ROSE.   How could she not know about it?

ABRAHAM LINCOLN.   I suppose we were just busy talking about other things.

ROSE.   Wonder how your friend would feel about my children.

ABRAHAM LINCOLN.   I can't rightly say. I am still trying to understand the lady's mind. But in any case she doesn't have children of her own.

ROSE.   Can't you imagine her feelings?

ABRAHAM LINCOLN.   As I say, Miss Todd is a bit unknowable.

ROSE.   She's a woman, Mr. Lincoln.

ABRAHAM LINCOLN.   Oh gosh, Rose. Listen, your children have a father, care to tell me about him?

ROSE.   Mr. Lincoln, you are curious.

ABRAHAM LINCOLN.   Well if you don't want to say...

ROSE.   *(Hesitantly.)* His name was Abraham, same as yours. Like me he was born here, on the plantation. One day about ten years ago, he was harvesting the hemp with the other slaves. Suddenly, a big horse reared up and knocked him down on top on one of those sharp hemp hooks...made of iron. *(Pause.)* He bled to death out there in the fields.

ABRAHAM LINCOLN.   I am sorry, Rose.

ROSE.   Sorry don't bring him back. I hear there are no slaves back where you're from.

ABRAHAM LINCOLN.   True. Slavery has been abolished in Illinois. Maybe someday they won't have it down here either.

ROSE.   You're wishing, Mr. Lincoln.

ABRAHAM LINCOLN.   I do that sometimes.

ROSE.   Come to think of it, we all do.

ABRAHAM LINCOLN. Maybe so. But tell me, what would you do if you were freed, say tomorrow?

ROSE. Why Mr. Lincoln, that's an easy one. I would go looking for my children.

ABRAHAM LINCOLN. As a mother would. I would hope you'd find them, but...

ROSE. Mr. Lincoln, you look sad. Maybe I spoke too much.

ABRAHAM LINCOLN. Oh, Rose, don't mind me. *(Pause.)* Look I've gotten a bit weary. Let us speak another time.

ROSE. Yes sir.

> *(Lincoln exits Stage Left. Rose moves off into the darkness and a single spotlight, as she sings: "Sometimes I feel like a Motherless Child")*

LIGHTS FADE

ACT ONE, Scene 3

AT RISE. Lights come up on the main Dining Room of Farmington. It is late Afternoon. Lucy, Joshua and Mary Speed are already seated at the long table set for dinner. Lincoln enters Stage Right, with a less rumpled suit.)

LUCY SPEED. Mr. Lincoln, you are looking better.

ABRAHAM LINCOLN. Well, thank you. Rose sure did a good job on my suit. I wish it could look this way when I wear it to the State Assembly.

MARY SPEED. Mr. Lincoln, I am sure you look very presentable on those occasions.

ABRAHAM LINCOLN. Why, Miss Mary?

LUCY SPEED. Mr. Lincoln, I am most anxious for you to meet my son James.

MARY SPEED. James lives downtown and is usually late.

ABRAHAM LINCOLN. I hear he has become quite a success as an attorney.

MARY SPEED. They are all seeking his services in Louisville.

LUCY SPEED. I am proud of James, but sometimes I wonder why they hire him with those radical ideas of his....imagine freeing the slaves.

MARY SPEED. Mother, James has his point of view.

LUCY SPEED. He wouldn't be where he is without our way of life here at Farmington. Does he realize that?

(Rose enters from the pantry, Stage Left.)

ABRAHAM LINCOLN. Hello, Rose.

ROSE. Mr. Lincoln, sir.

LUCY SPEED. Rose, I hope you've done your best cooking for Mr. Lincoln.

ROSE. Mrs. Speed, I did.

LUCY SPEED. We shall see.

ROSE. Mrs. Speed is never happy with my cooking, seems it never good enough for her.

LUCY SPEED. Rose!

ABRAHAM LINCOLN. It will be good enough for me.

JOSHUA SPEED. Probably so, I never knew Abraham to be picky about his food.

LUCY SPEED. I am sorry about all this commotion during dinner Mr. Lincoln. Now, Rose, please go down to the kitchen to get the roast mutton.

ROSE. Yes, ma'am. please.

(Rose exits.)

LUCY SPEED. I find Rose rather ungrateful for the good life we provide her.

JOSHUA SPEED. She's fortunate she wasn't sold to one of those plantations down in Mississippi.

LUCY SPEED. Had that happened, she'd wish she were back here.

ABRAHAM LINCOLN. I have heard say the lash of the whip is harsher down there.

LUCY SPEED. That is so true.

JOSHUA SPEED. Mother is right.

MARY SPEED. You see Mr. Lincoln, we're different from those folks way down south.

(James Speed enters the dining room.)

LUCY SPEED. Oh finally, here is James, late as usual.

JAMES SPEED. Good evening folks, forgive my tardiness, but I had to see a client at the last minute. Ahhh, I know this to be one Abraham Lincoln.

ABRAHAM LINCOLN. That it is, James. *(Stands to greet James.)* And I do know about those insistent clients.

LUCY SPEED. Please sit down James. Now that we are all here, let me ask who wishes to say grace?

(A moment of silence reigns at the table.)

LUCY SPEED. Hmmm, in that case... Bless this food to our use and us to thy service. Keep us ever mindful of the needs of others and those in our care. We pray thee for the coming harvest that it be bountiful. In the name of our Lord, Jesus Christ, Amen.

ALL. Amen.

(Lincoln looks out into space with a blank expression)

LUCY SPEED. Mr. Lincoln, I imagine you to be a religious man.

ABRAHAM LINCOLN. Well... Yes.

LUCY SPEED. Then Mr. Lincoln, I want you to know I am giving you an Oxford bible. I left it by your bedside. Reading it may assist you in overcoming that melancholy of yours.

ABRAHAM LINCOLN. That's mighty thoughtful of you Mrs. Speed.

JOSHUA SPEED. Mother, sometimes I've seen Abraham reading his tattered old bible in bed, late at night.

ABRAHAM LINCOLN. And I'll try reading this beautiful new one while I am here.

MARY SPEED. Oh, mother will be so pleased.

JAMES SPEED. Did I sense a little stir in the air when I came in? What in heaven's name were you all talking about?

LUCY SPEED. Now James, you've just met Mr. Lincoln. We are trying to keep the conversation pleasant.

JAMES SPEED. Of course mother. *(Pause.)* Mr. Lincoln, I would like to hear about your law practice?

ABRAHAM LINCOLN. I take almost any client I can find.

JAMES SPEED. And I understand you have stepped your foot into politics as well

ABRAHAM LINCOLN. Yeh, a little too deep. I'm feeling like an utter failure at the Legislature.

JOSHUA SPEED. Abraham has proposed extensive public works in Illinois.

LUCY SPEED. What might they be?

ABRAHAM LINCOLN. New railroad lines and a canal system.

MARY SPEED. Well that's something to be proud of.

JOSHUA SPEED. Why Abraham fashions himself another DeWitt Clinton. Personally I have my doubts about government expenditure on such things.

ABRAHAM LINCOLN. Joshua, I knew you and many others didn't want to pay more taxes, but I believed in what I did

MARY SPEED. Mr. Lincoln, of course you did.

ABRAHAM LINCOLN. But gosh, Illinois is bankrupt. And they blame it all on me

MARY SPEED. It's not all your fault, and besides the state will pull out of it.

ABRAHAM LINCOLN. No, it's a disaster. I'm afraid my political career is ruined.

(Lincoln gulps at his food.)

LUCY SPEED. Maybe I shouldn't say, Mr. Lincoln, but if you wish to succeed in politics, maybe you should think about your table manners. Didn't your mother teach you?

ABRAHAM LINCOLN. Mrs. Speed, my mother died when I was only nine. And then my sister and I were left alone.

MARY SPEED. All alone?

ABRAHAM LINCOLN. Father traveled back by himself to Kentucky to find a new wife.

LUCY SPEED. I am sorry about that. And your new mother, did she instruct you?

ABRAHAM LINCOLN. *(With a smile.)* Obviously not well enough.

JAMES SPEED. Mother, you are the one who wanted to keep the conversation pleasant.

JOSHUA SPEED. Lincoln, please, while dining, just look at me and do as I do.

ABRAHAM LINCOLN. Thanks, Speed. I'll watch closely.

MARY SPEED. You'll see, just like his suit, Mr. Lincoln's rough edges will iron out.

LUCY SPEED. I would like to think so.

MARY SPEED. Mother, let's have James tell Mr. Lincoln about his law practice.

JAMES SPEED. It's just the everyday practice of law, no politics.

ABRAHAM LINCOLN. Wise on your part.

JAMES SPEED. Maybe so. I will tell you much of my time is taken up with slavery matters, and they can be troublesome.

LUCY SPEED. I thought we were not going to talk about that.

MARY SPEED. No, let's hear more about what James does downtown. We live in such a small world here at the plantation.

LUCY SPEED. Mary, a lady should not be so inquisitive, it's unbecoming.

(Rose reenters the Dining Room.)

ROSE. Good evening, Master James.

JAMES SPEED. Why hello, Rose, something smells delicious .

ROSE. I heard you were coming Master James. You know I always like to cook special for you. And Mr. Lincoln is here.

JAMES SPEED. Well thank you, Rose.

ABRAHAM LINCOLN. And Rose, I appreciate the attention.

ROSE. You're welcome. Mr. Lincoln

LUCY SPEED. That will be enough Rose. You may leave.

(Rose exits)

JAMES SPEED. You know I always sense a tinge of sadness in Rose.

LUCY SPEED. I don't see why. She has every reason to be happy.

MARY SPEED. Mother, could it be her feelings are invisible to you?

LUCY SPEED. I hardly think that's possible.

JAMES SPEED. On the other hand, Morocco, from what I can see, seems content.

JOSHUA SPEED. He will find his good attitude has rewards.

ABRAHAM LINCOLN. Perhaps I am wrong, but Morocco didn't seem that happy earlier.

JOSHUA SPEED. That's just Bracker. He can be hard on him.

JAMES SPEED. Once in a while when he's sent downtown on errands, he drops over to the house and brings produce from your garden.

JOSHUA SPEED. Hmm, I didn't know that. Maybe he does dawdle around like Bracker says.

MARY SPEED. He always comes back soon enough.

JOSHUA SPEED. If you say so, but this kind of thing makes me worry about the slaves.

JAMES SPEED. Personally, I espouse the idea of sending them all back to Africa. To that new colony in Liberia. That would put an end to your worries, once and for all!

LUCY SPEED. You are incorrigible.

JOSHUA SPEED. Damn it, James, you've got to be out of your mind. What would I do here without the slaves, go back to my little store on the prairie?

JAMES SPEED. Can't you imagine a life without selling something Joshua?

JOSHUA SPEED. Hah, that's fine talk coming from a lawyer.
> (*Lincoln clears his throat and gently tries to change the direction of the conversation.*)

ABRAHAM LINCOLN. Joshua, you know I am one of those, umm, lawyers, too.

JOSHUA SPEED. To be sure.

ABRAHAM LINCOLN. And I studied mighty hard to be one.

JOSHUA SPEED. You know there's that vague belief that lawyers are necessarily dishonest.

JAMES SPEED. Is that so? From time to time, we do perform the valuable service of keeping dishonest merchants out of jail.

LUCY SPEED. Children...

MARY SPEED. Mother, Joshua and James, like any two brothers, can't be expected to agree on everything.

ABRAHAM LINCOLN. That's true, but let's end this discussion peacefully. May I have one last query. James, please tell me about that client you just saw.

MARY SPEED. I am curious about him too.

JAMES SPEED. He's an immigrant from Germany, John Bakrow, an owner of a dry goods store downtown. He puzzles me.

JOSHUA SPEED. Because he does honest work?

JAMES SPEED. Well, he wants me to represent him in the purchase of a slave. Surprising how quickly he's embraced our peculiar institution. I am disappointed that a man who's come to our country to escape tyranny and find freedom is so willing to put another man in bondage.

JOSHUA SPEED. He is a businessman, like myself. He is doing what he has a right to do. There's no law against it.

JAMES SPEED. The absence of a law doesn't make it right, Joshua, nevertheless, I shall represent Mr. Bakrow.

ABRAHAM LINCOLN. We lawyers have our job to do. You know, come to think of it, I once saw to it that a runaway slave was returned to his master.

(The Speed family members turn to Lincoln and stare quizzically.)

LUCY SPEED. What else should you have done, Mr. Lincoln? However, I want no more of this talk. We are serving peaches and cream for dessert, but you all have ruined my appetite. You can enjoy them by yourselves.

MARY SPEED. Mother, please stay.

LUCY SPEED. And why should I? Good evening, everyone.

(Lucy Speed gets up from the table and exits. The rest of them, for a moment, freeze up, and then start talking again.)

MARY SPEED. Seems we've never learned our lesson, have we? There are just certain things mother doesn't want to hear. You know our friend the famous composer, Anton Heinrich, is coming to Farmington in a few days, Mr. Lincoln, he was here when I was a little girl, so many years ago...he gave me my first lessons on the piano. Mother so adored him. Maybe his visit will put her in a better mood.

JOSHUA SPEED. I understand mother's feeling. We shouldn't have upset her so with all that talk.

JAMES SPEED. You're right. Why don't we make plans for your stay here?

MARY SPEED. That's a good idea.

JAMES SPEED. Well, I have a thought, why don't we all go out for a ride together. I'll have Morocco hitch up the thoroughbreds. I want to show you a place not far from here we call 'Big Rock" I won't tell you more now, but Abraham, you are going to be fascinated.

ABRAHAM LINCOLN.   That sounds mighty fine. I am looking forward to it.

LIGHTS FADE

ACT ONE, Scene 4

AT RISE. Lights slowly rise on Rose's bare wood slave quarters. She is pressing a heavy iron on a pile of laundry, as Morocco enters.

ROSE. So you come to help? That'd be the first time.

MOROCCO. I wanted to talk to you.

ROSE. What about?

MOROCCO. Bracker.

ROSE. He's just trying to show Master Joshua he's doing his job.

MOROCCO. No, no. It was the same even back when Master's father was alive.

ROSE. Oh, stop your crying, boy.

MOROCCO. Master Joshua just don't see it. He's all wrapped up in his own business.

ROSE. What you expect?

MOROCCO. Master Joshua has been pretty good to me. It's that Bracker I hate.

ROSE. You wake up. They own us like cattle. You might be sold tomorrow, and they wouldn't think one minute about your going away.

MOROCCO. I s'pose

ROSE. And I heard the way the men look over the slave women when they stand up on the auction block, half naked.

MOROCCO. I know about that, too.

ROSE. I cry to think of my daughter standing up there...

MOROCCO. Rose, don't let yourself think about that.

ROSE. How can I help it?

(Rose approaches Morocco and stares him in the eye.)

ROSE.   (CONT'D) You say Master Joshua's been good to you, but he's like all the rest. Like all the slave masters.

MOROCCO.   How is that?

ROSE.   He's the one who gives the orders to Bracker.

MOROCCO.   I can't know about that.

ROSE.   You don't know a lot of things.

MOROCCO.   One thing I do know, I can't take this life anymore.

ROSE.   What are you going to do about it?

MOROCCO.   Don't know. Nothing, I suppose. I'm trapped.

ROSE.   No you're not, there is another way.

MOROCCO.   What's that?

ROSE.   *(Pauses, then...)* Morocco...Run.

MOROCCO.   What did I hear?

ROSE.   I said run, boy. If you can get across the Ohio, you are a free man.

MOROCCO.   You damn house nigger. Telling me to run away, while you stay, living real sweet. Look at you, all dressed up like you're going to sit down at the table with 'em.

ROSE.   You will never see me do that.

MOROCCO.   Then you shut your mouth.

ROSE.   No. You're a young one. You've got a chance.

MOROCCO.   They'll tie me to the whipping post.

ROSE.   They'll whip you if you stay.

MOROCCO.   Rose, you talk big.

ROSE.   I say what I know.

MOROCCO.   I can't do it

ROSE. Don't be a coward.

MOROCCO. You're asking a lot.

ROSE. I know...

(Morocco stands back from Rose and stares straight in her eye, pause)

MOROCCO. I'll run...on one condition.

ROSE. Just what condition are you talking about?

MOROCCO. You come away with me.

ROSE. You're out of your mind.

MOROCCO. No Rose, I'll need you along the way.

ROSE. Need me?

MOROCCO. If we get across, it's gonna be a long hike to Ripley. Maybe a week. You'll help me gather something to eat, and do some cooking, and I won't be so lonesome.

ROSE. You're better off alone. They'll see the two of us before they see one.

MOROCCO. I'll take that chance. You gotta come with me Rose. You just tell me why not.

ROSE. Reasons.

MOROCCO. Like what?

ROSE. I'm too old.

MOROCCO. You told me you're only thirty-six.

ROSE. That's old.

MOROCCO. That's no reason.

ROSE. And besides, I can't swim.

MOROCCO. I'll get you across.

ROSE. No. I'll drown. I want to live to see my babies someday.
MOROCCO. You won't see them staying here.

(Rose breaks into tears. Morocco steps back looking helpless.)

ROSE. No, no. There's no good way.

MOROCCO. Look here, Rose, you changed my mind. Now you gotta change yours.

ROSE. I just wasn't thinking about anything like this.

MOROCCO. Rose...I've heard tell of a white man, named John Cerf. He ferries runaways across over near Harrod's Creek. Out where it opens up to the river.

ROSE. That's too far away.

MOROCCO. Come on. You've walked much further than that.

ROSE. They'll chase us with the hounds.

MOROCCO. Now, where's your courage, woman?

ROSE. Oh you're putting me to shame.

MOROCCO. Rose.

(Morocco embraces Rose sympathetically.)

ROSE. I hope someday my babies will be free and never be whipped again. I want them to walk proud.

MOROCCO. That the way it's going to be. Rose, you wait. You'll see 'em up North.

ROSE. I can't run while we have a guest.

MOROCCO. Why is that?

ROSE. It will spoil Mr. Lincoln's visit.

MOROCCO. You're talking nonsense. That just an excuse. Mr. Lincoln don't seem like the kind that would care.

ROSE. Come to think of it, maybe he would understand.

MOROCCO. Then tell me. Will you go with me?

(Rose steps back and looks up at ceiling, then stares at Morocco.)

ROSE. Oh Father in Heaven, what should I do?

(Morocco holds Rose's hand.)

MOROCCO. You know what to do.

ROSE. Morocco...

MOROCCO. Rose, let's leave this place...please.

ROSE. You sure?

MOROCCO. I am.

ROSE. Oh, let me think about it some more.

MOROCCO. No Rose, we're going cross that river.

ROSE. Oh my God, when?

MOROCCO. Tomorrow...after midnight.

LIGHTS FADE

ACT ONE, Scene 5

AT RISE. Lincoln and Speed are sitting side-by-side in rocking chairs on the front porch of Farmington. Speed smokes a cigar with a drink in his hand.)

JOSHUA SPEED. Lincoln, how about a little drink? Some of our fine Bourbon.

ABRAHAM LINCOLN. You know I never touch the stuff.

JOSHUA SPEED. I think you're missing something.

ABRAHAM LINCOLN. I claim no moral superiority. Just never had a yen for it.

JOSHUA SPEED. Maybe you are fortunate.

ABRAHAM LINCOLN. Yes. For some it creates great misery.

JOSHUA SPEED. I know. I do suppose I have to commend you for having no vices.

ABRAHAM LINCOLN. That is a doubtful compliment, Speed. I recollect once being on a stagecoach when another man from Kentucky sitting beside me offered me a seegar. I told him I had no vices. He said nothing, smoked for some time, and then finally grunted out, 'It's been my experience that folks who have no vices have damn few virtues.'

JOSHUA SPEED. Ha, ha,

ABRAHAM LINCOLN. Although it seems your sister Mary believes I have some virtues.

JOSHUA SPEED. It does seem that way. Anyway now you know my family a bit. Mother is the way she is, nothing to be done about that. And I have to admit, I do take after her. James is another matter altogether. As you can see he's gone his own way.

ABRAHAM LINCOLN. That's a family for you. I guess I'm the one in mine who went off on his own. Father wanted me to stay on the farm and lend a hand. But, I couldn't. I just wasn't cut out to be a farmer. Remember, back in Springfield, I left you and traveled to visit my father on his farm. We just didn't have much to say to each other.

JOSHUA SPEED. Fathers and sons. Never an easy thing.

ABRAHAM LINCOLN. You know, it's ironic, you are the one who's ended up on the farm. Though I can tell you, this place is nothing like my father's.

JOSHUA SPEED. Thinking back I do recall your taking that trip to see your father. Billy Herndon and Davis too were around, but it was still lonesome without you.

ABRAHAM LINCOLN. I was sure glad to come back and have you to talk to after those five days with father.

JOSHUA SPEED. I trust we will always have each other.

ABRAHAM LINCOLN. Do you really think so?

(Lincoln stands up and reaches for Joshua's hand.)

JOSHUA SPEED. Why do you worry?

ABRAHAM LINCOLN. What's happened in the past.

JOSHUA SPEED. What do you mean?

ABRAHAM LINCOLN. All the losses, do I have to name them?

JOSHUA SPEED. There is someone back in Springfield who loves you.

ABRAHAM LINCOLN. Yes...

JOSHUA SPEED. If you want her, you won't lose her.

ABRAHAM LINCOLN. Honestly, I am still as uncertain about Mary Todd as I was last December.

JOSHUA SPEED. It's understandable you broke off the engagement to Mary. My brother James rails against the chains of slavery, but Lincoln, isn't our argument with the chains of marriage?

ABRAHAM LINCOLN. Ha ha! Oh, Joshua, Mary is a wonderful woman. It depresses me so that I have hurt her. But I question if I love her enough to spend my life with her.

JOSHUA SPEED. That's something I've wondered too. I did observe a few of your sidelong glances over toward that pretty Matilda Edwards.

ABRAHAM LINCOLN. That's not it. It's not about anyone in particular.

JOSHUA SPEED. Really?

ABRAHAM LINCOLN. No. I am the problem. There are so many questions in my mind.

JOSHUA SPEED. Like what?

ABRAHAM LINCOLN. Just the very word 'marriage' frightens me. If I ever got married, it would be a matter of profound wonder.

JOSHUA SPEED. Oh come now.

ABRAHAM LINCOLN. How could I afford a family?

JOSHUA SPEED. Surely your law practice will prosper.

ABRAHAM LINCOLN. I can't see it. Besides, Mary Todd and I come from such different backgrounds.

JOSHUA SPEED. That I cannot deny.

ABRAHAM LINCOLN. You know one D is good enough for God, but evidently not for the Todds.

JOSHUA SPEED. Ha ha. Now it's your turn.

ABRAHAM LINCOLN. Mary would fit right in with you people.

JOSHUA SPEED. True enough. The Todds and Speeds have been friends from way back.

ABRAHAM LINCOLN. While I'm just a country boy.

JOSHUA SPEED. Married couples have a way of growing together.

ABRAHAM LINCOLN. Is there compromise in that?

JOSHUA SPEED. A natural one. Abraham, you seek an impossible happiness.

ABRAHAM LINCOLN. Ah, you know me. I yearn to walk across Elysian fields.

JOSHUA SPEED. Elysian Fields. I guess we are alike in that way.

ABRAHAM LINCOLN. In so many ways, my dear friend.

JOSHUA SPEED. To be quite honest, I find myself in a dilemma, something like yours. I have met a beautiful, young Louisville lady. Her name is Fanny Henning.

ABRAHAM LINCOLN. Should I be happy for you?

JOSHUA SPEED. I don't know.

ABRAHAM LINCOLN. Tell me more about this Miss Henning.

JOSHUA SPEED. Oh, she's has heavenly black eyes.

ABRAHAM LINCOLN. Well, I hope to meet her.

JOSHUA SPEED. You will.

ABRAHAM LINCOLN. Don't worry, I won't reveal what we've talked about.

JOSHUA SPEED. I certainly hope not.

ABRAHAM LINCOLN. I am always ready to assist in your romantic endeavors.

JOSHUA SPEED. I never thought I needed help, until now.

ABRAHAM LINCOLN. How is that?

JOSHUA SPEED. I just accused you…but you know how I was back in Springfield. I was drawn to so many pretty women myself and quite a few were drawn to me.

ABRAHAM LINCOLN. *(With a tone of sarcasm.)* Yes. I remember, you even took a glance or two at Sarah Rickard.

JOSHUA SPEED. Lincoln, I confess that was nothing serious. Now with Fanny it's different.

ABRAHAM LINCOLN. How so?

JOSHUA SPEED. I feel trapped.

ABRAHAM LINCOLN. Trapped? Now it's your turn to be.

JOSHUA SPEED. She wants nothing more than to get married.

(Mary Speed enters from the house onto the porch)

MARY SPEED. Did I hear talk of marriage?

JOSHUA SPEED. Mary, please sit down. Don't upset Abraham with your concerns.

MARY SPEED. I wouldn't do that.

JOSHUA SPEED. You have a way.

MARY SPEED. Don't be silly, Joshua. Mr. Lincoln, you're looking quite content this fine summer evening.

ABRAHAM LINCOLN. Miss Mary, settling in here at Farmington, I am beginning to feel a little better.

MARY SPEED. And, your being here has lifted my spirits.

(Lincoln is embarrassed again and attempts to divert the conversation.)

ABRAHAM LINCOLN. Miss Mary, I am, why...ahem, so pleased... *(Turning to Joshua.)* Joshua, I was curious about Rose. We had a little talk when she took me to my room.

MARY SPEED. That is surprising. Rose is very closed mouthed.

ABRAHAM LINCOLN. She was reluctant.

JOSHUA SPEED. You should have left her alone.

ABRAHAM LINCOLN. I sensed there was something she wanted to tell me.

MARY SPEED. What was that?

ABRAHAM LINCOLN. Those children she lost. That's made her so unhappy.

JOSHUA SPEED. *(Pointing to the end of the lawn.)* We do our best to keep the slaves happy. Well just look over there at the fine cabins we've built for them.

ABRAHAM LINCOLN. I don't know, Joshua. They look even worse than the ones I grew up in.

JOSHUA SPEED. Then your memory fails you.

ABRAHAM LINCOLN. It's only been five years since I lived in a log cabin in New Salem. I remember what they were like.

JOSHUA SPEED. Don't feel sorry for yourself.

ABRAHAM LINCOLN. I don't. But gosh, after seeing a mansion like Farmington. And then I look over at those slave cabins...The contrast, Joshua...

JOSHUA SPEED. It's the way it's always been.

ABRAHAM LINCOLN. If only it could be better?

JOSHUA SPEED. That's dreaming.

MARY SPEED. I am afraid you two are heading into a squall. Why don't we just talk about plans for tomorrow?

JOSHUA SPEED. Mary...ever the peace maker.

MARY SPEED. Listen Mr. Lincoln, James invited you to come downtown and have dinner with him at the Galt House Hotel about twelve-thirty. He dines there almost every afternoon. Afterwards, you can browse through his law library.

ABRAHAM LINCOLN. A fine idea. Maybe afterward I'll take a look around the city.

MARY SPEED. When you get back perhaps we can spend some time together. I propose we take a little walk across the hemp fields toward dusk, when it is not too hot.

ABRAHAM LINCOLN. Well, Mary, uh... Joshua might want to...

JOSHUA SPEED. No, it's ok. Lincoln, please go have dinner with James at the hotel tomorrow. And why not take that walk with Mary. Maybe I'll butt in toward the end.

MARY SPEED. You are certainly welcome to.

JOSHUA SPEED. Well thank you, Mary.

ABRAHAM LINCOLN. Yes, Joshua. Why don't you join us?

JOSHUA SPEED. We'll see. It's getting late, folks. Let me say good-night.

LIGHTS FADE

ACT ONE, Scene 6

AT RISE. The interior of the Galt House restaurant in Downtown Louisville. A table and chairs are set in a dimly lit stage, not immediately visible. Lincoln enters from offstage, in the spotlight, approaches the table and finds Mary Speed seated there instead of James as expected.)

ABRAHAM LINCOLN.   Why, Miss Mary. What are you doing here?

MARY SPEED.   I thought I would come downtown and have a little dinner. I was hoping I would run into you.

ABRAHAM LINCOLN.   This is a bit of a surprise. I was fully expecting to meet your brother James.

MARY SPEED.   Mr. Lincoln... to tell you the truth, James didn't know about an appointment. He is off working a case. I just felt I had to speak with you away from everyone else.

ABRAHAM LINCOLN.   I don't know what to say.

MARY SPEED.   You don't have to say anything. Please just hear what I want to tell you.

ABRAHAM LINCOLN.   Shouldn't we order some dinner first? I must say I am hungry.

MARY SPEED.   Oh I am sorry. I didn't consider that, Mr. Lincoln, oh, may I call you Abraham? I guess I am just wrapped up in my own thoughts.

ABRAHAM LINCOLN.   That alright, Miss Mary. But let me tell you, I am suffering from the worst toothache imaginable.

MARY SPEED.   Oh I am so sorry. Where is that troubling tooth of yours?

ABRAHAM LINCOLN.   Right here, Miss Mary.

MARY SPEED.   Oh. Let me order some of our fine Kentucky specialties for you. After dinner I'll give you the name of a dentist. Maybe you can get an appointment for later on.

ABRAHAM LINCOLN. That would be mighty nice of you. It's awfully painful, and I have had enough pain recently.

(A WAITER enters in formal attire.)

MARY SPEED. Maybe you recall some of our local food from your childhood.

ABRAHAM LINCOLN. That was a long time ago.

MARY SPEED. Waiter, please bring us a nice serving of burgoo, you know the Kentucky stew. It will be easy for you to eat with that tooth.

WAITER. Yes, right away, ma'am.

ABRAHAM LINCOLN. Burgoo? I don't remember it.

MARY SPEED. Just in case you don't like it... Waiter... some Kentucky ham with those greasy beans and yes, corn pudding. You know, Abraham, it's too hot for any more of that heavy mutton.

WAITER. Yes, ma'am. That ham is one of our specialties.

ABRAHAM LINCOLN. That sounds fine, except how about some more of those peaches and cream for dessert? They'll be easier too on this damned tooth of mine.

MARY SPEED. Most definitely, Abraham.

(Waiter exits.)

ABRAHAM LINCOLN. Thanks, now you just tell me what's sitting on your mind.

MARY SPEED. Abraham, life on the plantation is so cloistered. I've been living there such a long time. You know I will be forty soon.

ABRAHAM LINCOLN. You couldn't be.

MARY SPEED. Oh yes. Now that father is gone, I'm all alone with mother. You know she's not my real mother.

ABRAHAM LINCOLN. I have a stepmother too.

MARY SPEED. That's something we share, isn't it, Abraham?

ABRAHAM LINCOLN. You're right in a way. But my stepmother was so kind to me.

MARY SPEED. I wish I could say the same of mine.

ABRAHAM LINCOLN. But tell me, don't you feel less alone now that Joshua is back?

MARY SPEED. Not really. Joshua has come back to us, but he's so wrapped up with business affairs. And now he's become entranced with that Fanny Henning. Then there's the slaves, more than fifty of them swirling around me, but they don't make me feel any less lonely. I can't make up my mind about them. On that point, I guess I'm somewhere between Joshua and James. I know the slaves are necessary, but then I see them toiling and suffering. I have to admit, I'm torn.

ABRAHAM LINCOLN. Torn?

MARY SPEED. That's something I can't speak to mother about.

ABRAHAM LINCOLN. Have you tried?

MARY SPEED. No, mother's ideas about life at the plantation are as fixed in place as that statue over there. Of course I was living at Farmington well before she came, but she quickly settled herself right in.

ABRAHAM LINCOLN. I am beginning to get a sense of that.

MARY SPEED. Maybe there's something you don't sense.

ABRAHAM LINCOLN. What's that?

MARY SPEED. The slaves. We are always living with the fear they're going to run away, worse yet, rise up against us.

ABRAHAM LINCOLN. That's a frightful thought.

MARY SPEED. Sometimes I feel like running away myself...

ABRAHAM LINCOLN. I can understand that. I felt trapped at my father's home and ran away. Off to New Salem.

MARY SPEED. Life sounds tough in Illinois. There's no pretty, rolling countryside like we have down here in Kentucky. Joshua tells me it's as flat as one of Rose's pancakes, and all you see are cornfields stretching out to the horizon.

ABRAHAM LINCOLN. Nonetheless, I've grown a liking for the place.

MARY SPEED. You could give it up. Why not set up a little law practice downtown. Joshua would like that. Louisville is a booming river town. It has a future. You wouldn't have to compete with James. There's plenty of work down here for everyone.

ABRAHAM LINCOLN. I am already set up in Springfield, and with a partner. I can't just pull up stakes. I've already aggravated him enough this last season with my ups and downs.

MARY SPEED. Your work is not everything. Joshua has told me a bit about Mary Todd.

ABRAHAM LINCOLN. He has?

MARY SPEED. From what I hear, I have the sense she's not right for you.

ABRAHAM LINCOLN. Just what did Joshua say?

MARY SPEED. He said she was strong willed and real moody all at the same time.

ABRAHAM LINCOLN. That's not far from the truth.

MARY SPEED. I don't think you would be happy with a woman like that.

ABRAHAM LINCOLN. She sure put my mind into a fix last winter.

MARY SPEED. So give her up.

ABRAHAM LINCOLN. Gosh, Miss Mary, I've thought of it.

MARY SPEED. What I should do is buy a house in the city and get away from Farmington forever. If you came down, we could be friends. You know, we could meet like this, now and then, for dinner.

(Lincoln is embarrassed and taken back, clears his throat not knowing what to say.)

ABRAHAM LINCOLN. Miss Mary, I need time to think about all that. For goodness sake, haven't I had enough that's been tugging at me?

MARY SPEED. *(Affectionately)* You old fuddy-duddy.

ABRAHAM LINCOLN. Well, maybe I am.

MARY SPEED. But still you're a sweet man.

(James enters from offstage.)

MARY SPEED. Heavens, look who's coming into the dining room! Why it's brother James.

JAMES SPEED. Well, what do we have here? I wasn't coming in for dinner today. I was tied up back at the office, but then I thought I would drop by for a little something to eat.

ABRAHAM LINCOLN. I am glad you did.

JAMES SPEED. Doesn't it say in the Bible, 'thou knowest not what a day may bring!'

MARY SPEED. *(Sheepishly)* You know James, I come downtown from time to time, and I thought it would be nice for Abraham to see the hotel. I don't suppose there is anything like this where he's from.

ABRAHAM LINCOLN. Yes this place is astonishing. Just look at those crystal chandeliers, that marble fireplace.

MARY SPEED. Do you see what I mean James?

ABRAHAM LINCOLN. Miss Mary and I have had a very interesting conversation, James. She's given me some insights.

JAMES SPEED. Well, good. I am glad to see my big sister getting out around town. In my opinion, Mary, you should do more of the same.

MARY SPEED. James, you are so right, but mother tries to keep me tied on the plantation. Why don't you have a few words with her on my behalf?

JAMES SPEED. I'll have to work up some nerve for that. Anyway, I am really tickled to see you two together.

MARY SPEED. *(Smiles)* Why don't you two wander off to your office, I know Abraham wants to browse through your law books. Morocco will be driving down to pick me up so I'll be just fine.

ABRAHAM LINCOLN. About that dentist?

MARY SPEED. Oh yes. James, see if you can make an appointment with Dr. Yates for Abraham.

JAMES SPEED. You've got to be jesting. The last time I saw Yates, he pretty much ruined my mouth.

ABRAHAM LINCOLN. I have become pretty accustomed to ruins. That's what my life is these days.

MARY SPEED. Abraham, stop it.

ABRAHAM LINCOLN. Well I'll just have to trust to luck with Dr. Yates.

JAMES SPEED. You'll need to.

ABRAHAM LINCOLN. Ahhh, James let's do walk over to your office. And Mary, many thanks. I'll be seeing you this evening.

LIGHTS FADE

ACT ONE, Scene 7

AT RISE. Two days later, early in the morning at Farmington. Lucy Speed, Mary Speed and Lincoln have gathered on the porch waiting to go in for breakfast. Joshua Speed enters with news.)

JOSHUA SPEED. Folks, there's no one to cook breakfast. Rose ran away last night. And Morocco ran with her.

LUCY SPEED. What?!

MARY SPEED. I don't believe it.

ABRAHAM LINCOLN. What happened?

JOSHUA SPEED. Bracker and Jake chased them down by Harrods Creek. Jake caught Morocco but he broke away. That's when Bracker shot him in the leg. They dragged them both back here about two in the morning.

LUCY SPEED. What will we do without them? You know my estimation of Rose, but still, we have no one who can replace her. And just when Mr. Lincoln is visiting.

MARY SPEED. Mother, I'll help as best I can.

JOSHUA SPEED. Doctor Jenkins said they might have to take off Morocco's leg. As if I haven't had enough losses.

MARY SPEED. I can't bear to hear anymore. Mother, please let's go down to the kitchen and prepare some breakfast for Abraham.

LUCY SPEED. Oh my goodness gracious, I can't remember when I ever cooked anything.

MARY SPEED. We'll make do.

ABRAHAM LINCOLN. Mrs. Speed, please don't go to much trouble for me.

(Lucy and Mary exit as Bracker enters pulling Rose along with him.)

HIRAM BRACKER.   Rose, I always thought you to be a good slave. I'll bet Morocco talked you into this.

JOSHUA SPEED.   Quiet, Bracker.

ABRAHAM LINCOLN.   Where is Morocco?

HIRAM BRACKER.   He's down in his cabin. We've got a watch on him.

ABRAHAM LINCOLN.   What about that leg?

HIRAM BRACKER.   Don't you be concerned.

ABRAHAM LINCOLN.   Why shouldn't I?

JOSHUA SPEED.   Leave Morocco be for now.

HIRAM BRACKER.   If he could stand up I'd give him a good whippin'.

JOSHUA SPEED.   Bracker! What did I tell you about whipping? We'll punish Morocco another way.

ROSE.   That's not fair, it was my idea to run.

JOSHUA SPEED.   Rose I've known you since you were a young girl. We've always trusted you.

ROSE.   I thought I could find my babies.

JOSHUA SPEED.   How did you get that idea into your head?

ROSE.   Morocco said I would.

HIRAM BRACKER.   If Morocco said anything like that I'll...

JOSHUA SPEED.   Rose you have sense enough to know that's impossible.

ABRAHAM LINCOLN.   Speed, don't you think we should get the facts.

JOSHUA SPEED.   This is a plantation, not one of your courtrooms.

ABRAHAM LINCOLN.   Still no reason to rush to a verdict.

JOSHUA SPEED.   Well I am going to think this over. Don't think that Rose is going without punishment too. Bracker, take her back to her cabin. Keep an eye on her as well.

ROSE.   Mr. Speed, have mercy. I only wanted to see my children. Honest I did. I'll never do it again.

JOSHUA SPEED. You betrayed me.

ROSE. I didn't mean to Master Speed. Now, I'll never see my Jacob and Eliza again.

JOSHUA SPEED. You don't deserve to. Get her away from me!

   (Bracker drags her offstage.)

ROSE. *(Anguished.)* Master Speed, Master Speed, what are you going to do to me?!

CURTAIN

END OF ACT ONE

ACT TWO, Scene 1

AT RISE. (At dawn: the stage is dark. The sound of a whip followed by a woman's scream is heard two times off stage.)

HIRAM BRACKER. I've never whipped a slave woman.. I can't go on.

(The lights brighten. Abraham, Lucy and Mary are seen standing in front of the house. Rose is tied to a tree. Joshua is holding the whip and is about ready to strike.)

MARY SPEED. Joshua, what are you doing?!

JOSHUA SPEED. Mary, stay out of this!

ABRAHAM LINCOLN. I can't believe what I'm seeing.

JOSHUA SPEED. You stay out of this too, Lincoln.

ABRAHAM LINCOLN. No, Speed, I can't.

JOSHUA SPEED. Listen to me. I don't want to do it. I told Bracker to punish Rose, but the bastard put the whip down after two lashes. It's his job, but if he won't do it, damn it, I will!

LUCY SPEED. Joshua, I think your father would have agreed.

(Lincoln grabs the whip from Joshua's hand.)

ABRAHAM LINCOLN. Did it occur to you that your man Bracker found an ounce of mercy this time?

JOSHUA SPEED. Rose deserves this.

ABRAHAM LINCOLN. You told me there would be no whippings at Farmington.

JOSHUA SPEED. I changed my mind.

ROSE. Ughhh. my God, ohh...

ABRAHAM LINCOLN. Rose.

ROSE. Please, Mr. Lincoln, free me..

JOSHUA SPEED. Leave her be.

ABRAHAM LINCOLN. Speed, I don't recognize the man I once knew.

JOSHUA SPEED. Returning here I see things differently.

ABRAHAM LINCOLN. And now so do I.

JOSHUA SPEED. This is the only way to treat these...

ABRAHAM LINCOLN. Human beings.

JOSHUA SPEED. Human beings that belong to me.

ROSE. Oh, please, please untie me!

JOSHUA SPEED. No, you are just going stay tied.

ABRAHAM LINCOLN. There's your slavery.

JOSHUA SPEED. You're damned right.

ABRAHAM LINCOLN. We'll all be damned.

JOSHUA SPEED. It's right that they be enslaved.

ABRAHAM LINCOLN. Maybe they're not our equals in every way. But don't they deserve to be treated decently?

JOSHUA SPEED. And just what makes you think you and I are equals?

ABRAHAM LINCOLN. Speed, I've never heard you say anything like that.

JOSHUA SPEED. I'm sorry, Lincoln, we are not equals. You said it yourself, you grew up in log cabins. How could you possibly understand everything about me? We can talk endlessly about poetry and our love problems. Everyone has those, but this is another matter.

ABRAHAM LINCOLN. I thought you saw more in me than that backwoods boy. I guess I was wrong.

JOSHUA SPEED. You were.

ABRAHAM LINCOLN. Well, Speed, maybe I better just go back to where I came from.

JOSHUA SPEED. You do as you wish. I was born here, and coming back to Kentucky, I have found a way of life I love... and now I intend to keep it.

ROSE. Master Joshua, I did wrong this time, but I was a good slave all those years. You forget that. Forgive me...please.

JOSHUA SPEED. I can't.

ABRAHAM LINCOLN. You are insufferable.

JOSHUA SPEED. I don't want to hear anymore from you!

ABRAHAM LINCOLN. If only you could hear yourself.

ROSE. Mr. Lincoln, I am feeling...

(Mary rushes to Rose in an effort to untie her.)

LUCY SPEED. Mary, leave her be.

MARY SPEED. Mother, have you no feelings?

(As Rose is let free, she takes a few steps forward and collapses. Mary hovers over her.)

MARY SPEED. Please, mother. Fetch some water.

LUCY SPEED. If I must.

(She exits.)

ABRAHAM LINCOLN. Mary, let's take her back to her cabin.

(Lincoln and Mary support Rose and leads her off stage.)

ROSE. Bless you, Mr. Lincoln...and Miss Mary.

LIGHTS FADE

ACT TWO, Scene 2

AT RISE. (Four days later, the stage is lit on the interior of Rose's Cabin. Rose is lying face down on a bed. Lincoln sits in a chair beside her.)

ABRAHAM LINCOLN. Not long ago I found myself lying in bed sore with wounds. I too had been whipped.

ROSE. You were whipped?

ABRAHAM LINCOLN. Wasn't the slave master's whip. It was with the cruel vicissitudes of life.

ROSE. Mr. Lincoln, what are… *(Says the word haltingly.)* …vicissitudes?

ABRAHAM LINCOLN. Changes. Some for the better. Many more for the worse. But I don't want to bother you with my troubles… You've had enough of your own.

ROSE. Lord, that is true.. Master Joshua didn't have to pick up that whip Bracker lashed me twice already… I I was hurting enough. Master Joshua has known me since we were children. We never had any trouble, but this time something new came out of him.

ABRAHAM LINCOLN. Something I couldn't understand either

ROSE. Master Joshua is just a part of this damn place.

ABRAHAM LINCOLN. A place I don't belong.

ROSE. Mr. Abraham, you don't.. You should go soon. Soon as you can. *(Pause.)* Mr. Lincoln, do you ever think about the future?

ABRAHAM LINCOLN. I am not sure I have one.

ROSE. I'm the one who has no future. But you do. You're free.

(Morocco enters on crutches with his leg bandaged.)

MOROCCO. Why, Mr. Lincoln. I didn't expect to find you here.

ABRAHAM LINCOLN. I came to cheer up Rose. I am glad to see you didn't lose that leg.

MOROCCO. So is Master Speed. He plenty mad at me, but he's mighty pleased I'm going to be back to work.

ABRAHAM LINCOLN. Work. That's all you are for, in Mr. Speed's mind.

MOROCCO. Truth to tell, I have some bit of respect for Mr. Speed. It's Mr. Bracker I hate.

ROSE. Yeah, would you respect Master Speed had he whipped you?

MOROCCO. I guess not.

ROSE. It was Mr. Bracker who showed some mercy. At least on me.

ABRAHAM LINCOLN. Morocco, open your eyes. It was Master Speed who grabbed the whip after Bracker put it down.

MOROCCO. I don't care, Bracker is a coward. Overseers are just that way. They're empty. They have nothing inside, so they go driving us slaves like animals.

ABRAHAM LINCOLN. I don't mean to defend Bracker...

MOROCCO. You can't.

ABRAHAM LINCOLN. It's Mr. Speed I'm angry with.

MOROCCO. You can be angry all you want. Maybe you don't know him well enough.

ABRAHAM LINCOLN. You would think I would after rooming with him for about four years...sharing the same damn bed.

MOROCCO. Don't mean you really know him.

ABRAHAM LINCOLN. I supposed my eyes were closed.

MOROCCO. Like his father before him, Master Speed tries to be fair.

ABRAHAM LINCOLN. Is that so?

MOROCCO. He cares about the plantation.

ROSE. Master Speed is a slave like us to the plantation...to the money it brings in.

MOROCCO. Like it or not, we're all in the business with Master Speed. You've got to know, Mr. Lincoln, I don't want to be a slave. Christ, I wished I had escaped, but as long as I have to be here, I'll work. If the plantation goes down, we all do. What would happen then? We would all be driven to another plantation where things probably be worse.

ABRAHAM LINCOLN. If you're so stuck to this life, why didn't you ever find a woman to have a family with?

MOROCCO. Mr. Lincoln, I am a slave and I can't help that; but I can and I will help being the father of any other slaves.

ABRAHAM LINCOLN. I can understand that.

MOROCCO. But it's good to have friends. You and Mr. Speed are friends...or were. Leave him if you will, but let me tell you Mr. Lincoln, there are no friendships that give you everything. There is always something missing.

ABRAHAM LINCOLN. How is that?

MOROCCO. There's Joseph. We like to tell stories together down here in the cabins, but damned if he will ever give me an extra hand in the stable when I'm tired.

ROSE. Yeah, that's Joseph.

MOROCCO. I just have to accept him as he is.

ABRAHAM LINCOLN. There are limits to that.

MOROCCO. Sir, you are all bothered up.

ROSE. He sure is.

MOROCCO. We've just been down to hell, but we have got to come back. Live right here and be as cheerful as we can be.

ABRAHAM LINCOLN. Cheerful? Yes, you folks can be that way. Morocco, when you met me at the docks, I saw twelve slaves, like yourselves, being led onto a boat to be shipped down river.

MOROCCO. Yeah. I remember.

ABRAHAM LINCOLN. Those slaves were chained six and six together. A small iron clevis around the wrist of each and fastened to the main chain like...like so many fish upon a trout-line. Yet it seemed that amid all that distress, they were cheerful. Singing and cracking jokes.

MOROCCO. That they were.

ABRAHAM LINCOLN. Isn't it true, Morocco, God tempers the wind to the shorn lamb?

MOROCCO. What do you mean by that?

ABRAHAM LINCOLN. I mean. he makes the worst of human conditions tolerable, while he permits the best - which I admit mine is - to be nothing but agony.

LIGHTS FADE

ACT TWO, Scene 3

AT RISE. (That evening in the parlor of the house. Lincoln sits alone, brooding in the dark, as Joshua enters.)

JOSHUA SPEED. Are you going to be angry forever?

ABRAHAM LINCOLN. I don't know what to say. *(Stares off into space, still brooding.)* I was so looking forward to coming. Now I can't wait to leave.

JOSHUA SPEED. Lincoln...

ABRAHAM LINCOLN. Slavery was always something I just brushed up against. Now I have run right into its center.

JOSHUA SPEED. What did you expect coming down here?

ABRAHAM LINCOLN. It wasn't on my mind.

JOSHUA SPEED. Who are you to judge me? What I see from you is ingratitude. Look what I have done for you. I gave you a room to sleep in. I introduced you to the best of Springfield society. I let you pour your heart out to me. And when you couldn't even get out of that bed, sick with the hypo, I was there for you. You might even have killed yourself, had it not been for me.

ABRAHAM LINCOLN. I am grateful for all that... Still, I am going to leave on the next boat I can book.

JOSHUA SPEED. Well, you will have time to think that over. There won't be one for another week.

(Lucy Speed enters the room.)

LUCY SPEED. Goodness, are you two still fighting?

JOSHUA SPEED. Mother, it's nothing. Just a little philosophical disagreement.

LUCY SPEED. It doesn't sound that way.

JOSHUA SPEED. Lawyer Lincoln argues strenuously. Even minor cases.

LUCY SPEED. Oh, Abraham, this is no time to argue. Old Mr. Heinrich has finally arrived. We should all be happy. I did not want to bring him into the parlor with this ruckus going on.

JOSHUA SPEED. You'll like Mr. Heinrich. He'll match you for a laugh or two.

LUCY SPEED. We certainly need a change of mood.

JOSHUA SPEED. True, but Mr. Heinrich has a curmudgeonly side. I remember how he would lose his temper when little Mary made mistakes on the piano.

LUCY SPEED. Joshua, Don't be nasty. I am going to invite him in. Anton!

(Anton Heinrich enters the room, speaking with a middle European accent)

ANTON HEINRICH. Hello, folks. I am so happy to be here again. But where is that pretty Mary?

LUCY SPEED. You'll see her a little later.

ANTON HEINRICH. Oh good, my favorite student. *(Turning to Lincoln)* I don't remember this one.

LUCY SPEED. This is our guest. Mr. Lincoln.

ANTON HEINRICH. Lincoln, hmmm. That name re-so-nates. Could you be from the distinguished Lincoln family of Rhode Island? I once gave a piano recital in their home.

ABRAHAM LINCOLN. Well, uh...

LUCY SPEED. I hardly think so.

ANTON HEINRICH. In either event, a young one you are. I was about your age when I came here last. Everyone knew of me then. It was the height of my career. My music was played everywhere. They even likened me to the great Beethoven. For God's sake. Look at me now. An old broken down...

ABRAHAM LINCOLN. You seem a lively spirit.

ANTON HEINRICH. Oh sure, hah!

LUCY SPEED. Anton, you will always be famous in our family.

ANTON HEINRICH. It is nice to be somewhere I am appreciated.

LUCY SPEED. That you are. Now please excuse me, I am going to let you men talk amongst yourselves. I have so many chores to do now that we don't have Rose. I admit, none of the other slaves can manage as she did. I am afraid it will be weeks before she recovers.

(Lucy Exits.)

JOSHUA SPEED. Lincoln, wait till you hear Anton play.

ABRAHAM LINCOLN. I can't say I know much about classical music, but I have tried my hand at poetry. I'm no Lord Byron, but I take pleasure in penning a line or two.

JOSHUA SPEED. It was I who introduced you to Byron.

ABRAHAM LINCOLN. I do owe that to you.

ANTON HEINRICH. Byron, exactly, an idealist! There aren't too many of those these days.

(Lincoln stares off into space, pensively crosses the stage and back and begins to recite one of his own poems.)

ABRAHAM LINCOLN. Here's one of my very own: "Memory! Thou midway world. Twixt earth and paradise Where things decayed and loved ones lost...'

JOSHUA SPEED. Oh stop it, how could you be in a mood to spout poetry.

ANTON HEINRICH. *(Cuts him off.)* Let him continue! I knew I saw something of the artist in this young man. A romantic spirit like myself.

JOSHUA SPEED. And he has the temperament to go along with it...or I should say the temper.

ABRAHAM LINCOLN. Are you trying to be funny?

JOSHUA SPEED. I am not certain I meant to be.

ANTON HEINRICH. For sure, you two are different creatures. But Joshua, in Mr. Lincoln here, do I not detect a touch of the melancholy typical of our artistic breed?

JOSHUA SPEED. He does his share of brooding.

ANTON HEINRICH. Joshua I can remember you last time I was here, the little tyke that you were. You did a bit of brooding when you didn't get your way.

JOSHUA SPEED. I confess, I like to get my way. But it seems you two have more in common. I am going to leave you brooding artists to commune amongst yourselves.

ANTON HEINRICH. Please, don't feel you are unwanted amongst us troubadours.

JOSHUA SPEED. No, I am leaving. You have no say in the matter.

(Joshua exits.)

ANTON HEINRICH. Mr. Lincoln, I sense you and Joshua are not getting along.

ABRAHAM LINCOLN. Yes, we have had a bit of a row.

ANTON HEINRICH. Ah, isn't this life filled with strife?

ABRAHAM LINCOLN. Never ending.

ANTON HEINRICH. I don't even want to know what the fight was about. Perhaps it doesn't matter.

ABRAHAM LINCOLN. It does to me.

ANTON HEINRICH. Should it really? It's a cliché, but life is short, and friends are hard to find. Even harder to keep.

ABRAHAM LINCOLN. Speed was the only really close friend I have ever had.

ANTON HEINRICH. That's something not to throw aside.

ABRAHAM LINCOLN. Speed did something reprehensible. We had been as close as two men can be, but in an instant, I no longer recognized him.

ANTON HEINRICH. People are different, they come from different countries, different cultures, different religions ... different races. Horrible wars have been fought over this stuff, and you can be sure, there are more to come. I'll bet you and Joshua were fighting a little war in miniature that will someday be a big one.

ABRAHAM LINCOLN. I hope that is never the case.

ANTON HEINRICH. I know what I say. Look here young man, I come from the old country where there have been wars for centuries, over nothing worth killing. Every little petty province is up in arms against the next. That's one reason I left. Alas, only to find more of the same here.

ABRAHAM LINCOLN. Sometimes there are principles worth fighting for.

ANTON HEINRICH. But the one between you and Joshua, whatever the hell it was, was it one of them?

ABRAHAM LINCOLN. It seemed so to me.

ANTON HEINRICH. Is there no way you can find mutual understanding? A compromise perhaps?

ABRAHAM LINCOLN. No, Mr. Heinrich, not this time.

ANTON HEINRICH. I can see this is useless to pursue further. Your mind is made up.

ABRAHAM LINCOLN. Thank you, Mr. Heinrich.

ANTON HEINRICH. You are velcome.

ABRAHAM LINCOLN. Tell me, you implied there were other reasons you came to America.

ANTON HEINRICH. Opportunity, of course. In Europe, composers like me were plentiful. You needed to find a patron in the nobility to get support, and I had no success with that.

ABRAHAM LINCOLN. In this country we believe in taking a man for his worth...if he has talent and works hard.

ANTON HEINRICH.   Whatever I did, I just wasn't valued as I should have been. Yet here they adore my music. At least they did. Alas my music has gone out of style. They are always looking for something new in this country. Constant change. I can't keep up with it...old age is catching up.

ABRAHAM LINCOLN.   I know that feeling,.. yet I do not have your years.

ANTON HEINRICH.   Anyway, you know Abe, I understand my old friend from Germany, John Bakrow, immigrated to Louisville. I hear he is one of James' clients. Now there is a man of culture, discernment, who appreciated my artistry. Unfortunately he was of little means, and couldn't aid my career.

ABRAHAM LINCOLN.   That's a shame.

ANTON HEINRICH.   Tomorrow I am paying him a visit. I hope he has a good piano for me to play.

ABRAHAM LINCOLN.   They tell me he has become quite wealthy. For goodness sakes, he's even buying a slave. I would imagine he will have a fine instrument in his home.

ANTON HEINRICH.   I'll tell you what, I am going to play for you one of my compositions. It's plain to see, you too are a man of discernment... You are head strong, but you have a big soul. I am convinced you will like what you hear.

(Heinrich begins to play one of his outrageous compositions. After a minute or so, the MUSIC FADES.)

LIGHTS FADE

ACT TWO, Scene 4

AT RISE. (In the parlor of the house. Lucy Speed, Mary Speed and Abraham Lincoln are gathered.)

LUCY SPEED. Abraham, I saw you left the Bible on the hall table.

ABRAHAM LINCOLN. Mrs. Speed, how can I accept your gift? I mean no disrespect, but what I have seen is hardly in accord with what I understand to be its teachings.

LUCY SPEED. Where does the Bible say slavery is wrong?

ABRAHAM LINCOLN. I don't know. But I do know it teaches mercy and justice.

LUCY SPEED. Enough of that. I gave you the Bible to help you.

ABRAHAM LINCOLN. I don't know that the Bible was intended as a cure for the blues.

LUCY SPEED. In any case, you have been a slave to your own petty tribulations. Everyone has those, but it seems you just can't bear up.

MARY SPEED. Melancholy is not a fault, mother. It's just Abraham's misfortune.

LUCY SPEED. I disagree. I can see Abraham has a gift, but he can do much more for himself, and get on with his life.

ABRAHAM LINCOLN. I shall try.

LUCY SPEED. You do just that. Maybe I'll see you at supper.

(Lucy Speed exits leaving Lincoln and Mary Speed alone.)

MARY SPEED. Oh, Abraham, mother does really care about you...and so do I.

ABRAHAM LINCOLN. Your mother is a tough lady, but I respect her.

MARY SPEED. I'm glad for that.

ABRAHAM LINCOLN. Mary, haven't we become something of cronies?
MARY SPEED. Cronies?

ABRAHAM LINCOLN. You know what I mean, really good friends.

MARY SPEED. Ah. Perhaps then it is time we had another one of our talks.

ABRAHAM LINCOLN. What more can we say? I have to leave.

MARY SPEED. Mother is right in some ways. You're taking it all too hard. You should understand that Joshua is conflicted. He really doesn't want to harm anyone, even our slaves. But he feels obliged to preserve our prosperity. Believe me, my brother is a good man.

ABRAHAM LINCOLN. Are you saying that I have to look at this in two ways? That's been required of me in politics, but I always have to decide.

MARY SPEED. You have to decide.

ABRAHAM LINCOLN. I am going back alone.

MARY SPEED. But a valuable friendship is at stake.

ABRAHAM LINCOLN. Not as valuable as I thought.

MARY SPEED. Even with all that has happened, you can't erase the closeness between you. I've learned to hang on to whatever is still there.

ABRAHAM LINCOLN. I don't think I can this time.

MARY SPEED. Who knows what's coming. You may find you need each other someday. Oh, Abraham, if it's the slavery issue that's troubling you, bear in mind, it's not going to be resolved anytime soon. Maybe never.

ABRAHAM LINCOLN. I fear you're right.

MARY SPEED   Listen, Abraham, Joshua didn't invent slavery.

ABRAHAM LINCOLN. But he's perpetuating it.

MARY SPEED. Has it ever occurred to you that somewhere deep down, he struggles with it?

ABRAHAM LINCOLN. That's something he doesn't reveal.

MARY SPEED. We can't know those closest to us. Not in every way.

ABRAHAM LINCOLN. You know Morocco told me the same thing. A wise young man he is. He made me think of my friendship with Billy Herndon back home. Billy only sees one part of me. *(Softly)* Maybe I only see part of him... I confess from time to time that Billy and I have had some fights.

MARY SPEED. Don't those quarrels get smoothed over and forgotten?

ABRAHAM LINCOLN. You say that, Mary. Remember that big rock down by the creek James took me to see? It makes me think of the friendship I had with Joshua. It must have been one hell of a piece of rock, but when it fell from the cliff, it split in two. Now there's that big ugly crack down the middle.

MARY SPEED. Two human beings are not a rock.

ABRAHAM LINCOLN. You don't give up.

MARY SPEED. I just want you to stay.

ABRAHAM LINCOLN. I am grappling with it.

MARY SPEED. Oh stop being wishy washy.

ABRAHAM LINCOLN. I hope you don't hate me for it.

MARY SPEED. At times, I have felt like committing assault and battery on you, but still I have a regard for you... You know I have gained a new perspective on our friendship.

ABRAHAM LINCOLN. You have?

MARY SPEED. I have to admit I thought it could be...more.

ABRAHAM LINCOLN. *(Gently.)* I must say I noticed.

MARY SPEED. I suppose it was apparent.

ABRAHAM LINCOLN. Oh, Miss Mary.

MARY SPEED. You are a wonderful man, Abraham, but you're at an uncertain point in your life.

ABRAHAM LINCOLN. Can't deny that.

MARY SPEED. When you have greater clarity, you are going to move on with conviction. One thing I know, your world is elsewhere. Not here. Not with me or Joshua.

ABRAHAM LINCOLN. Miss Mary, my sense is you will stay in Louisville. Good things are going to happen for you.

MARY SPEED. I wonder... But whatever happens, just your being here now has made me feel less lonely.

ABRAHAM LINCOLN. And knowing you just a short while...

(Knocking is heard at the parlor door. Joshua Speed enters.)

JOSHUA SPEED. I've lost a friend, but I see you've gained one.

MARY SPEED. Joshua, please talk to Abraham. Persuade him to stay.

JOSHUA SPEED. I don't think he wants to talk to me.

ABRAHAM LINCOLN. We can share some parting words.

MARY SPEED. Oh Abraham!

(Rose stumbles on. Still bent over in pain from the whipping.)

JOSHUA SPEED. Rose, you can't come in here.

ROSE. Master Speed, I wanted to say goodbye to Mr. Lincoln. I knew he was going to leave and let me tell you, I think he should.

JOSHUA SPEED. Do you want another..?

ROSE. Nothing more can hurt me.

MARY SPEED. Rose, this is not the time.

ABRAHAM LINCOLN. Rose, I appreciate it, but for everyone's sake, be calm.

ROSE. How can I be?

ABRAHAM LINCOLN. This is something Mr. Speed and I have to work out.

JOSHUA SPEED. Rose, go back to your cabin!

ROSE. No, I want to see Mr. Lincoln go away from here. Miss Mary, I know what you want, but you've got to think what's best for Mr. Lincoln.

MARY SPEED. You think you know what's best for him?

ROSE. I do know. He's got to go right away...on his own path, alone.

JOSHUA SPEED. Rose, leave this room, or I will drag you out of here!

ROSE. No, I won't.

JOSHUA SPEED. Rose, I said leave!

(Speed grabs Rose and forcibly pushes her out the parlor door. Rose shrieks as she is pushed off stage. Lincoln and Speed stand face-to-face, staring darkly at each other.)

ABRAHAM LINCOLN. Speed, that was your chance to show some mercy!

JOSHUA SPEED. Look, Lincoln. I am not entirely the brute you think I am.

(Lincoln sits down with his head in his hands.)

JOSHUA SPEED. *(CONT'D.)* I know you are man of principle. Maybe to a point of fault. But you have to be flexible in politics...and friendship too..

ABRAHAM LINCOLN. In politics, I set limits, knowing how far I can bend. Despite what you may think, I make compromises.

JOSHUA SPEED. Keep that in mind.

ABRAHAM LINCOLN. Don't tell me what to think.

JOSHUA SPEED. I can't get anywhere with you.

ABRAHAM LINCOLN. Look I need to get away from this place. I am going downtown tonight, by myself, away from you all. I'll check into the Galt House and wait there for the next boat, for as many days as it takes.

JOSHUA SPEED. Have it your way.

ABRAHAM LINCOLN. Joshua, I have to do that. But when that boat finally comes, I'll expect...

JOSHUA SPEED. What?

ABRAHAM LINCOLN. ...that you'll join me at the docks to travel back.

JOSHUA SPEED. Together?

ABRAHAM LINCOLN. Yes.

MARY SPEED. Oh, Abraham, I hoped you would say that.

ABRAHAM LINCOLN. You two had me pushed to the wall.

MARY SPEED. It's sad you are going, but you will be leaving us with memories.

ABRAHAM LINCOLN. I will have my own.

MARY SPEED. Abraham, promise me you will write me a letter when you get back to Illinois.

ABRAHAM LINCOLN. I promise.

JOSHUA SPEED. Lincoln, I'll be there at the docks to meet you...I think the steamboat Lebanon is due in six days.

MARY SPEED. Abraham, you will be on an uncertain journey again.

ABRAHAM LINCOLN. Yes, it has been a journey these last three weeks. And I have to say, despite everything that has happened, I have been given a greater sense of myself - a strange new energy.

JOSHUA SPEED. At least something has come of it.

ABRAHAM LINCOLN. Well then, guess I best pack my satchel and get on with it.

JOSHUA SPEED. Lincoln, you take care of yourself down there all alone at the hotel.

ABRAHAM LINCOLN. Don't worry, I'll have some time to reflect. Now let me go say goodbye to Mr. Heinrich and your mother. I am going to tell her that I'll put that Bible in my satchel.

MARY SPEED. Oh, she will be so pleased.

ABRAHAM LINCOLN. I hope so.

MARY SPEED. Goodbye Abraham.

ABRAHAM LINCOLN. Goodbye Mary.

(Mary kisses Abraham and exits.)

JOSHUA SPEED. It's going to be a tedious trip back. Maybe we can do a little talking along the way, get to know each other again.

ABRAHAM LINCOLN. I can't imagine things will be the same.

JOSHUA SPEED. Yes, but I just hope our friendship doesn't fade away... completely.

ABRAHAM LINCOLN. Indeed, Joshua. If we have no friends, we have no pleasure, and if we have them, we are sure to lose them.

JOSHUA SPEED. That's a sad thought

ABRAHAM LINCOLN. So true. How miserably things seem to be arranged in this world of ours.

(The LIGHTS DIM and the stage remains darkened for several moments. Lincoln ambles off, leaving Joshua on stage alone.)

EPILOGUE

AT RISE. Lights come up full on Joshua Speed standing in front of the closed curtain, reminiscent of his appearance in the Prologue.

JOSHUA SPEED. Lincoln and I did return on that boat together. Back in Springfield, we no longer roomed together, and after a few months I returned to Louisville permanently. In the course of year 1842, we exchanged some rather intimate letters concerning our respective considerations of matrimony. After Lincoln married Mary Todd later that year, our letters became few and far between, mostly about business matters. I regret that when Lincoln visited Lexington in 1847 to stay with his in-laws, on his way to congress in Washington, he didn't even stay with us at Farmington arriving in Louisville as he did. We only saw each other many years later in 1860 at Chicago just after he was elected President. I have to say I am grateful he invited me to the White House many times during the war to advise on the troubling situation in Kentucky. In particular, I recall one visit in 1865 toward the end of the great battle...

> *(The Curtain opens to reveal a small room in the White House. It is twenty-four years later and Speed and Lincoln seated together before a cast iron fireplace. Both men now have beards; Lincoln has his iconic stovepipe hat positioned on a table nearby. He is finishing a passage in the Bible before setting it aside.)*

JOSHUA SPEED. *(CONT'D.)* Is that the Bible mother gave you years ago?

ABRAHAM LINCOLN. Yes it is. And I remain in debt to her.

JOSHUA SPEED. I am glad to see you so profitably engaged reading it.

ABRAHAM LINCOLN. Yes, I am profitably engaged.

JOSHUA SPEED. Well, if you have recovered from your skepticism, I am sorry to say I have not.

> *(Lincoln stands and places his hand on Speed's shoulder.)*

ABRAHAM LINCOLN. I never knew you to be a skeptic, but if you have so become, you are wrong. Speed, take all of this book upon reason that you can, and the balance on faith, and you will live and die a happier and better man.

JOSHUA SPEED. After what has happened these last four years, it is hard to feel any real happiness.

ABRAHAM LINCOLN. Despite all the killing, something has been accomplished for which I believe posterity will be grateful. It appears our Union has been saved and slavery...

JOSHUA SPEED. You know full well I had always believed in the rightness of that institution. As of late, I have come to reconsider. After much reflection, I suppose I have come closer to your point of view. *(Pause.)* Anyway, it hardly makes a difference. Slavery is soon to be abolished everywhere, whatever I had thought...or think now.

(A knock is heard at the door.)

ABRAHAM LINCOLN. Come in.

(Morocco enters.)

MOROCCO. Mr. President, Mr. President! There's good news coming from Virginia!

ABRAHAM LINCOLN. Let's hope there is more, Morocco. But let's not celebrate yet.

JOSHUA SPEED. Mr. President, has Morocco been of assistance to you?

ABRAHAM LINCOLN. Indeed he has.

MOROCCO. I have been trying my best, sir.

ABRAHAM LINCOLN. Speed, it was an act of great generosity, your freeing Morocco and sending him up here to help out at the White House.

JOSHUA SPEED. It's made me feel much better.

MOROCCO. Heavens, to think I'm here in the White House! What an honor. And what a thrill it was to see Mr. Frederick Douglass dining with President Lincoln.

ABRAHAM LINCOLN. Frederick does make an impression.

MOROCCO. You may not believe it, but I do miss Farmington. Often wonder how Rose is doing.

JOSHUA SPEED. Morocco, I thought I told you, she can no longer work.

MOROCCO. What's she been doing then?

JOSHUA SPEED. Rose spends her time down in her cabin by herself.

MOROCCO. I knew it would come to that.

JOSHUA SPEED. You know there are happenings in life that cause everlasting pain.

MOROCCO. I feel that pain, too. Don't know I deserve to be here, when she's back there all alone.

ABRAHAM LINCOLN. From time to time, I think of Rose myself... my visit to Farmington seems so far in the past.

JOSHUA SPEED. Mr. President, you know as well as I do, as I predicted our friendship has faded. But still, I have been trying as hard as I can to help you save the Union. We've become like two government employees. Well for sure you have the better job. Maybe this can be a turning point back to where we were those many years ago...around that old potbelly stove in my store.

ABRAHAM LINCOLN. Are you saying a friendship too could be saved?

JOSHUA SPEED. That's my hope.

ABRAHAM LINCOLN. I know you feel that way, and I'm appreciative. But right now Speed, I am a little alarmed about myself, just take my hand.

(Speed reaches over and grasps Lincoln's hand.)

JOSHUA SPEED. My goodness, it's so cold and... clammy.

ABRAHAM LINCOLN. What could be wrong?

JOSHUA SPEED. You're just suffering from overwork. Terribly so.

ABRAHAM LINCOLN. I suppose I ought to be in bed.

JOSHUA SPEED. Take care of yourself. Please.

MOROCCO. President Lincoln, he's so right.

ABRAHAM LINCOLN. No I must labor on until this wretched war is completely won.

MOROCCO. Don't you worry sir, it will be soon enough.

JOSHUA SPEED. Yes, that is certain.

ABRAHAM LINCOLN. Speed, Mary and I have talked about a long vacation after this term is up, maybe even a trip to France.

JOSHUA SPEED. That would do you good. I wish it could happen sooner.

ABRAHAM LINCOLN. Yes. Mary has always wanted to see Paris.

MOROCCO. For now, Mr. President, why don't you just step over to that fire I made for you, and warm those hands?

ABRAHAM LINCOLN. Thank you, Morocco. I think I'll do just that.

(Lincoln stands and walks across the stage to the fireplace.)

ABRAHAM LINCOLN. *(CONT'D.)* Ah, this warm fire is such a comfort...

(The light follows him and then dims. The stage darkens completely. After a momentary pause the stage is lit again with Joshua Speed standing alone again on the stage.)

JOSHUA SPEED. Lincoln never took that vacation he needed so badly. Sad it was that our friendship never progressed beyond where it was that dreary day, early in spring. That was the very last time I saw him. *(Takes a solemn step forward. Pauses.)* Two weeks later on April 14th, Good Friday, Abraham Lincoln was shot dead…

CURTAIN

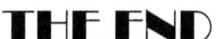

DAVID S. TRAUB, JR.

Lincoln In Louisville premiered at the The Alley Theatre in Louisville, Kentucky in June, 2015 in commemoration of the 150th Anniversary of the end of the Civil War, the assassination of Abraham Lincoln and the passage of the 13th Amendment ending slavery everywhere in the United States

ORIGINAL CAST

Joshua Speed	Daniel Smith
Abraham Lincoln	Scott Davis
Mary Speed	Collette Delaney
Lucy Fry Speed	Teresa Wentzel
Morocco	Keith McGill
Rose	Courtney Cleveland
Hiram Bracker	Michael Montgomery
James Speed	R. Wayne Hogue, Jr.
Anton Heinrich	Sean Childress
Director	Vin Morreale, Jr.
Stage Manager	John Cosper
Set Design	Camille Cothron
Lighting & Stage Assistants	Kelly Craddick
	Carrie Faulhaber
	Leslie C. Langford, Jr.

The following have been of immense assistance in the creation of this production of **Lincoln in Louisville**: Dr. Charles B. Strozier; Frank Friday ,Esq.; *Contributing Writers were* Thom Nickels, Patricia DiStefano and Leslie Miller. Special acknowledgement is due Ed Shockley who was instrumental in guiding the playwright through early drafts of the play.

Lincoln Quotes Used in the Play

The following are some of the actual quotes, or paraphrases thereof, by Abraham Lincoln used throughout the play:

"Your words are encouraging, but I still have done nothing to make anybody remember that I have lived."

"When I arrived at the docks here in Louisville, I saw a gentleman who had purchased twelve negroes in Kentucky leading them onto a boat traveling south. They were chained six and six together, a small iron clevis was around the wrist of each and fastened to the main chain by a shorter distance from the other, so that that the negroes were strung together precisely like so many fish upon a trot-line."

"It would seem the negros can't be made our political and social equals. You know our own feelings would not admit of that, and if I could come around to that myself, the rest of our other white friends surely wouldn't.."

"I am the most miserable man alive!"

"I don't doubt that the Bible is the best cure for the blues, if we could only take it according to the truth."

"You know, Anton, last week I had to shut her (Mary Speed) up in a room to prevent her from committing an assault and battery upon me."

"I know you agree with me how miserably things seem to be arranged in this world of ours. If we have no friends, we have no pleasure; and if we have them, we are sure to lose them, and be doubly pained by the loss."

One of Abraham Lincoln's Poems:

"O, Memory! Thou midway world
Twixt earth and paradise
Where things decayed and
loved ones lost
In dreamy shadows rise,
And, freed from all that's vile,
Seem hallowed, pure, and bright,
Like scenes in some enchanted isle
All bathed in liquid light."

Notes on the Play

While the play employs dramatization, it is loosely based on historical fact. In instances, some events from the past and future are compressed forward and back into the time of the 1841 visit. The writer takes this liberty in order to portray Lincoln, the man, his evolving thinking on slavery, and the narrative of his ongoing friendship with Joshua Speed, as it extends to the end of Lincoln's life.

Anton Philip Heinrich (1781-1861) was a historical figure. He was born in Bohemia and immigrated to the United States where he worked as a composer. He visited the Farmington Plantation giving piano lessons to Mary Speed in the 1820's. He was called the "Beethoven of America."

John Bakrow is the Great Great Grandfather of David S. Traub Jr. He immigrated to Louisville from Germany in the late 1830's and reportedly owned one slave.

Matilda Edwards was a cousin of Ninian Edwards, the brother-in-law of Mary Todd. Like Lincoln and Joshua Speed, she was a member of the elite social circle that gathered in the Edwards' Springfield mansion. There has been speculation that both Lincoln and Speed had a romantic interest in Matilda, however never substantiated.

Sarah Rickard likewise was a member of the Edwards' social circle. She too was a subject of speculation about Lincoln's and Speed's romantic interests.

The "hypo" was an expression Lincoln and his contemporaries used for a depressed state of mind.

John Cerf, another ancestor of David S. Traub, Jr., reportedly helped operate the Underground Railroad in Louisville.

Ripley, Ohio was an important station along the Underground Railroad, just across the Ohio River from Kentucky southeast of Cincinnati.

Historical Background

For three weeks, in August and September of 1841, Abraham Lincoln visited his friend Joshua Fry Speed at Farmington, Speed's plantation home at Louisville, Kentucky.

Though born in Kentucky, by the year 1837 Lincoln was living in Springfield, Illinois, where he had just launched his legal career. Joshua Speed was also living in Springfield, having left Kentucky for this newly developing state to strike out on his own away from his wealthy family. Lincoln and Speed met that year of 1837 and it is generally considered that Joshua Speed became the best friend Lincoln ever had. It is well documented that they roomed together above Speed's general store for almost four years, sharing the same double bed. On the frontier, it was very common for men to share beds. Nonetheless, this fact has led to speculation about Lincoln's sexuality though there is no evidence available that indicates that Lincoln and Speed were anything but friends. The playwright's contention is that Lincoln and Speed in the 1840s indeed were loving friends, but that theirs was not a sexual relationship.

In one of his many letters to Speed, Lincoln wrote, "You know my desire to befriend you is everlasting." Later Speed said of his friendship with Lincoln, "no two men were ever more intimate."

When Speed finally left Springfield for good, Lincoln remarked in a letter to Speed, "I shall be very lonesome without you. How miserably things seem to be arranged in this world! If we have no friends, we have no pleasure; and if we have them, we are sure to lose them, and be doubly pained by the loss."

At the same time, Lincoln was considering settling down, courted several Springfield women and finally became engaged to Mary Todd, still another Kentuckian living in Springfield. Mary Todd came from a prominent, aristocratic Lexington family. She was well educated, spoke French and possessed all of the polite, social skills. Both Speed and Todd, with respect to their backgrounds, were the exact opposite of Lincoln, who, as we all know, was born in a log cabin and had hardly any formal education.

(Separate paragraph) Around January 1, 1841, Lincoln, for reasons that remain ultimately unclear, broke off his engagement to Mary Todd. Concurrently, his intimate friend Speed, his father having died, was called back to Kentucky to manage

the plantation with its 50 or so enslaved Afro-Americans. And to make matters worse, Lincoln had suffered setbacks in his legal and political career.

During the winter of 1841, perhaps, as a result of the thought of all these occurrences interacting in his mind, Lincoln became seriously depressed, even suicidal. Lincoln himself recognized his depression and sought medical attention in Springfield with Dr. Anson Henry who effectively served as his psychiatrist. Lincoln used the then current expression, the "hypo," to identify his depression.

In a letter he wrote to his then law partner, John Stuart, he confessed that "I am now the most miserable man living. If what I feel were to be distributed to the whole human family, there would not be one cheerful face on the earth. Whether I shall ever be better I cannot tell; I awfully forebode I shall not. To remain as I am is impossible; I must die or be better, it appears to me."

Speed remembered that Lincoln had stated at the time of his depression that "he was more than willing to die, but that he had done nothing to make any human being remember that he had lived, and that to connect his name with the events transpiring in his day and generation and so impress himself upon them as to link his name with something that would redound to the interest of his fellow man, was what he desired to live for."

Lincoln's depression did ease somewhat as the months wore on, but not completely, as Speed discerned from news he received from Springfield.

While these events were taking place in Lincoln's personal life, Joshua Speed was courting a lovely Louisville lady, Fanny Henning. Speed too was uncertain as to proceeding into marriage, and the consideration of their respective marriage propositions was the subject of much discussion and subsequent correspondence between the two men.

This is the background that led up to Speed's invitation to Lincoln to come down to the plantation for a restful and hopefully curative visit. The three week stay was probably the longest period of leisure that Lincoln ever enjoyed. David Herbert Donald, perhaps the leading Lincoln scholar of our time, has written: "In that spacious mansion, built by skilled Philadelphia artisans around 1809, he experienced a life of leisure that he had never known before....all in all, it was a most successful vacation." One of Lincoln's happy memories of the visit was being served peaches and cream at the Speed dinner table. However, it seems Lincoln was embarrassed by the Speed's displeasure with his table manners as he consumed the peaches and other culinary delights offered in the plantation dining room.

During the visit, according to David Donald, Lincoln was assigned a personal slave to attend him, though this fact is in question. With Joshua, he took long walks or rode on horseback across the fields and woods of the plantation. Speed's mother, Lucy, doted over him giving him a bible as a gift, hoping that reading it would relieve his despair. He traveled to downtown Louisville to visit Joshua's brother, lawyer James Speed, in his office where he studiously read law books. Years later as president, Lincoln appointed James Speed his attorney general in his second administration.

While in Louisville, Lincoln availed himself of its health care establishment. We know from Lincoln's correspondence with Joshua Speed's sister, Mary, that he had a tooth pulled by a local dentist who was an amateur photographer. Some think this dentist may have taken the first photographic image ever taken of Lincoln, a daguerreotype. Regarding his mental condition, he seems to have consulted one of the foremost physicians practicing in America, Dr. Daniel Drake of Cincinnati, who also had an office in Louisville at the time of the visit.

Of significance is that Lincoln's visit to Farmington was probably the first time he saw slavery in action. He had visited New Orleans twice, about ten years earlier, where he had observed slave markets, but at Farmington, he was living in the midst of a working southern plantation with slaves toiling all about him in the fields and house. Although Lincoln's position regarding slavery at that time was by no means fully formed, he was dismayed by the spectacle of slaves chained together on the riverboat sailing down the Ohio to St. Louis en route back to Illinois. Lincoln and Speed did not agree on the issue of slavery, and although they returned to Springfield together in September of 1841, their friendship, perhaps owing in part to this difference, was never again as close as it had been at Farmington and the three months they spent together in Springfield after their return from Kentucky. When Lincoln returned to Kentucky to visit Mary Todd's family in Lexington, he reportedly did not stop to visit Speeds at Farmington.

As it turned out, while Lincoln subsequently experienced other episodes of depression, none were as severe as the one in 1841. Certainly there were other events in his later life to be very depressed about, but the Louisville sojourn did seem to lead to an elevation of his spirits that continued to sustain him. Lincoln returned to Springfield, resumed his legal and political career, resolved to marry Mary Todd the following year and started a family. Hardly seven years later, in 1848, Lincoln found himself in Washington, DC as an elected congressman from the State of Illinois. If Lincoln had gone no further in his political career, this in itself would have been a significant accomplishment, given the events of the few preceding years.

In summary, we consider Lincoln's visit to Louisville one of several pivotal moments in Lincoln's life. The visit served to clarify his friendship with Joshua Speed, a relationship crucial to his passage into maturity. After the visit, Lincoln began to see the way clear to marry Mary Todd and establish a household. The visit also marked the beginning of a period in his life in which he was able to successfully manage his tendency to experience debilitating episodes of depression. Finally and importantly, the visit was his first hand encounter with slavery operating all around him,, reinforcing an aversion to this terrible institution which he had held from childhood, and which of course was to become a center piece in his future political career.

After the visit despite setbacks, disappointment and tragedy, Lincoln persevered, forging ahead on his path to ultimate success. In 1861, only twenty years after his 1841 visit to Louisville, Lincoln finds himself in the White House.

An interesting footnote is the fact that many consider that the architectural design for Farmington, though prepared by a local architect, may have been based upon plans by Thomas Jefferson, one of Lincoln's heroes, who was acquainted with the Speed's maternal ancestors in Virginia. Farmington, therefore, is a house associated with two great American presidents.

Legend has it that Abraham Lincoln and Joshua Speed, in the course of the 1841 sojourn, together visited Big Rock which is located in Louisville's Cherokee Park.

About The Playwright

David S. Traub, Jr. is a Philadelphia-based playwright, author, and architect.

Born in Louisville, Kentucky in 1941, his early childhood was spent in a house that in 1841 was on the grounds of the Farmington plantation. In August 1841 Abraham Lincoln visited Joshua Speed for three weeks at his plantation. Traub had often imagined that Lincoln and Speed during the sojourn rode on horseback across what later became his front yard. In 2006 these imaginings gave rise to his idea for the play *Lincoln in Louisville*, produced in 2015 at Louisville's Alley Theatre.

Traub has more recently written a play, *Woodford Place*, a dramatization of his childhood growing up in Louisville presented also at the Alley Theatre in 2018. Another of his plays, *Train to Essex Junction*, is scheduled for production in 2021.

www.ingramcontent.com/pod-product-compliance
Lightning Source LLC
Chambersburg PA
CBHW071029080526
44587CB00015B/2545